I0090240

ADHD ADULT
Women

Manage Chaos, Empower Focus, Stay Tuned,
and Become More Productive in Your Life in
Natural and Easy Steps.

Margot T. Lewis

© Copyright 2024 by Margot T.Lewis - All rights reserved.

This document is geared towards providing exact and reliable information in regard to the topic and issue covered.

- From a Declaration of Principles which was accepted and approved equally by a Committee of the American Bar Association and a Committee of Publishers and Associations.

In no way is it legal to reproduce, duplicate, or transmit any part of this document in either electronic means or in printed format. All rights reserved.

The information provided herein is stated to be truthful and consistent, in that any liability, in terms of inattention or otherwise, by any usage or abuse of any policies, processes, or directions contained within is the solitary and utter responsibility of the recipient reader. Under no circumstances will any legal responsibility or blame be held against the publisher for any reparation, damages, or monetary loss due to the information herein, either directly or indirectly.

Respective authors own all copyrights not held by the publisher.

The information herein is offered for informational purposes solely and is universal as so. The presentation of the information is without a contract or any type of guarantee assurance.

The trademarks that are used are without any consent, and the publication of the trademark is without permission or backing by the trademark owner. All trademarks and brands within this book are for clarifying purposes only and are owned by the owners themselves, not affiliated with this document.

Table of Contents

Introduction

A lot of people are familiar with the disorder from their childhood. However, the pattern is also often seen in adults who have ADHD and experience similar symptoms.

Adult women who have ADHD are thought to be three times more likely to suffer from depression and anxiety during their lifetime and be more likely to develop sleep disorders or substance abuse problems. They may also endure stress during pregnancy which can cause accidental injury or harm to their baby's development.

Those with ADHD may find themselves living with a significant amount of pain, unable to perform everyday activities like work and caregiving that they once did without any issue. They may struggle with relationships, especially romantic ones, and feel like they cannot make steady progress toward goals.

Sometimes, they can function fairly well in certain areas of their lives, but struggle with other aspects. In other cases, the disorder interferes with almost every area of an adult woman's life.

The symptoms include inattention, hyperactivity and impulsivity behaviors, which may be accompanied by low self-esteem or affect relationships with others. Approximately one in ten women who have ADHD are diagnosed with an anxiety disorder like social anxiety disorder or panic disorder. They also are likely to be more likely to seek medical treatment if they experience pain with their physical health issues than other adults who have ADHD.

This pattern of behavior isn't just seen in adults, however. ADHD is often thought of as a behavioral disorder that affects children only. However, about 5% to 10% of children will develop ADHD as adults as well. Although symptoms may change as the child ages and intellectual development progresses, the condition doesn't disappear.

Some signs that an adult woman has ADHD include repetitive behaviors like tapping a foot or having trouble concentrating on one thing for long periods of time or issues with organization and memory. These are typically accompanied by difficulty completing tasks and difficulty performing certain types of social interactions.

Although ADHD is a condition that is treated with medication in most cases, it can be difficult to get an accurate diagnosis without the proper tests. Most women who have ADHD have had previous diagnoses that they don't believe are accurate.

ADHD is an abbreviation for attention-deficit/hyperactivity disorder. It's a brain disorder characterized by restlessness, impulsiveness and difficulty concentrating on tasks that require sustained focus.

There is no known answer to when and where this disorder started. The condition appears to have been created quite early in human history. There are many different theories on how this disorder came into being. One of them is that ADHD was a mixture of other mental illnesses that may have been combined over time.

There is also the chance that men were simply the first to develop ADHD. They were exposed to high levels of dopamine at an earlier age than women because they are significantly more physically active than women as a whole.

There are many theories and misconceptions about adult ADHD. Not much is known about ADHD in women, but it is still an important topic. Women with ADHD often find themselves struggling more than men because of how society perceives them, their different symptoms and the treatments available for them. Adult women with ADHD can find themselves feeling isolated, unsupported, or frustrated by the disorder.

The exact cause of ADHD is not clear, and it may be that there are several reasons for the symptoms. Similarly, exposure to drugs, alcohol or other chemicals during pregnancy may cause ADHD in the mother. While these environmental factors are possible causes, research suggests that different brain areas appear to be affected by the disorder.

Studies have shown that women with ADHD have more trouble with planning and organization, another symptom of the disorder. Studies have shown that 60 percent of untreated ADHD in adults is due to depression, anxiety, or a chemical imbalance in the brain.

This book talks about the different symptoms of ADHD in women. It also talks about how society perceives them and the various treatments available for them. ADHD impacts women more than men because societal norms are not as accepting of their types of symptoms. If you are feeling isolated, unsupported, or frustrated because of this disorder, this book will open you up to strategies that will help you get better.

If you are an executive or have a high-stress job, you may have to concentrate very hard on the tasks at hand and may have trouble shifting your focus away from work when you go home. As a result, chores around the house often get neglected until it's too late, and you find yourself drowning in dirty dishes and laundry.

Women with ADHD tend to be more sensitive to stress than men and have consistent difficulty managing their emotions. Women with ADHD also commonly have problems with time management, adapting to change and following instructions. In addition to these symptoms, some women report that they feel numb towards life. Others report feeling emotionally abandoned by loved ones when their ADHD was not recognized or appropriately managed.

Generally, this book is suitable for both men and women. However, the central focus is on women who are more prone to this disorder. I would recommend that women with ADHD read this book, as it may provide some helpful insights into the condition and how to deal with negative emotions.

PART I - Understanding ADHD

Chapter 1: What is ADHD

ADHD stands for Attention Deficit Hyperactivity Disorder. It's a chronic neurological disorder that affects about 11% of children between the ages of 4 and 17 in the United States, making it one of the most common mental disorders in children. The symptoms are difficult to control, often causing significant problems with social relationships, academics, work performance, and self-control. If you have Adhd you're more likely to have trouble sleeping at night because your thoughts are constantly racing through your head or if you get overloaded taking care of your responsibilities then sudden mood changes can happen throughout the day. This is quite a troubling disorder because without treatment many people who have ADHD struggle their whole lives to find success.

ADHD must be diagnosed by a professional in order to receive appropriate treatment, but some practitioners are better at finding accurate diagnoses than others. Many of these professionals are referred to as "experts" rather than psychologists, but that doesn't mean they aren't trained in validating ADHD as a legitimate condition. There are several different types of ADHD presentations that can affect executive function and response to medication, and there's more to the condition than just hyperactivity and impulsivity. It's vital to get a complete picture of your child's presentation so you can help him or her feel better about his or her situation.

Many people who have ADHD have hyperactive-impulsive symptoms that cause inattention as well. It's a common presentation that can cause considerable underachievement in school, and it often leads to social problems as well.

Inattention is one of the most common symptoms of ADHD in adults, but people with hyperactive-impulsive symptoms also have problems concentrating and planning ahead. This means they're often less likely to get through college or complete work at a high level, and it can result in difficulty getting a job that is more than cleaning or serving customers.

Many people with these symptoms have an endless amount of energy but may lack the ability to focus on one thing for long enough to get anything done. A person with ADHD may be adept at cleaning a room, but if the task is boring or too taxing, he or she will get distracted and move onto something else.

Getting the right treatment can help with symptoms and help people with ADHD learn to differentiate tasks that require more concentration from those that don't. While medication can be effective for hyperactivity and impulsivity, talking therapies can help with inattention as well.

The symptoms of inattention can look a lot like the symptom of underachievement. The difference is one of degree.

For example, a child may be able to answer questions in class and volunteer to answer them correctly, but she might not understand them or know how to apply the information that she's learning. She may be able to do her homework without any help and even get all of her assignments finished on time, but they might be incomplete or poorly done. This is often due to either a cognitive problem or an overreaction to stress—or both.

A child who has ADHD will need to have this addressed in order to succeed in school, though medication might be helpful with the underlying symptoms of impulsivity and hyperactivity.

Proactive symptoms show up as problems with starting tasks or finishing them properly. You might notice that your child doesn't seem to know where things are in their room or wallet, or they might have trouble getting out the door on time. This can result in frustration and a sense of failure that spreads to other areas of life and can keep a person from succeeding socially as well as academically.

Being disorganized can also impact people's emotions. Organization can help people manage their time and plan for the day ahead.

Many people who struggle with the organization have trouble focusing on one thing for very long because there are always too many things to look at or worry about. It's important to keep your attention focused on one task and get that finished before moving onto something else.

If your child is struggling with these symptoms, it's important to talk to them about their thoughts and feelings. Asking questions like "What are you thinking about right now?" can help your child learn about their thought process. This can help you help them break the cycle of failure, disorganization, and stress that keeps them from succeeding in school or gaining a higher level of education than their current situation would seem to warrant.

Does ADHD Ever Go Away?

Ah, the joys of having ADHD. You know it's a laundry list of obstacles: social stigma, economic difficulty, inability to focus on anything for long periods of time... The list goes on and on. But you're not alone! In fact, about 10% of women in North America have this condition; there's no need to feel weird about it anymore.

And the good news is that yes, ADHD can go away. It's not a lifelong curse, and it's not a death sentence. The bad news? It can take time.

ADHD is a condition that affects many women, but it is not

exclusive to women. Adults with ADHD have trouble with focus, organization, time management, and impulse control... And the disorder is marked by hyperactivity in childhood and a tendency toward inattention when they're older. Adults who have grown up with the effects of this disorder often struggle to deal with it; for some people, it's debilitating in relationships and career paths.

But, like we said before, ADHD can go away. That's the good news.

The bad news? It takes time, effort, and energy to manage it effectively. It also takes patience — you probably won't see results overnight. (Although you might be surprised by how much things change.) But it is worth the effort. You just need to be patient.

ADHD is not a death sentence, and it doesn't mean your child cannot be successful. Educate yourself about the disorder, and reach out to your local mental health organizations for more information. And don't forget to ask your doctor! The best way to understand a disorder like this is by getting the professional input that you need. ADHD can be managed with the correct treatment; when you seek help, you can eliminate this condition's challenges. It's worth it in the end — so take care of yourself today!

Is ADHD Inherited?

If you have a family history of ADHD, there is a potential that you're more likely to develop the condition. That's why it's essential to know the signs of ADHD to get help quickly.

Much of ADHD, if not all of it, is inherited. A study done at Lafayette College in the United States found that in a sample of 700 adults with ADHD given a diagnosis by physicians, 95% had relatives with ADHD in their family history.

A study done at MIT came to the same conclusion about how much is inherited. The study found that "47 percent of women diagnosed with ADHD have an immediate family member also diagnosed.

A study in Australia used both parents and women to measure ADHD in the family. The study concluded that 75% of the time, if both parents and women have ADHD, the child will have ADHD too.

The authors of this study said that "these findings indicate that a wide range of individually rare conditions can be quite common within families."

This means that multiple members of a family can share many common problems. For example, there are many cases where one parent has depression or anxiety while another parent is having trouble keeping a job. The women in this family will have a much higher chance of having depression or anxiety and job problems.

A parent's emotional state can contribute to an ADHD child's emotional state. In the case of one study, high levels of cortisol, the stress hormone, were found in women with high levels of anxiety.

This might not be genetic, but can be caused by a stressful environment where parents are arguing a lot or involved in other stressful events like a divorce. The situation is stressful for the child and will cause them to have more cortisol than normal. Increased cortisol can cause ADHD like symptoms.

There are several other factors that may contribute to ADHD in women. These include prenatal alcohol exposure, environmental toxicants such as lead, and maternal infections, nutrition and obesity before and during pregnancy. There are many other possible causes of ADHD that need to be taken into consideration if a child has ADHD.

One of the issues with ADHD is that there have been some cases where people have faked symptoms in order to get attention. One study found that 5% of the sample had malingered ADHD. This means that they lied about having ADHD in order to receive special treatment, which was seen as a positive result of their actions.

The only way to tell if someone has faked their ADHD diagnosis is a neuropsychological assessment by a highly trained professional. This is an expensive process and may not be worth it if the person isn't going to be seeking any professional help for his or her symptoms.

In 2006 it was reported that over 50% of people who used psychostimulants for at least six months had received a diagnosis of ADHD by professionals. The reasons for the high rate of self-diagnosis are unknown.

As the use of ADHD medications increases, side effects such as weight loss and insomnia have become issues for many people who take them without understanding what they are putting into their bodies.

There is also a myth that ADHD is caused by poor nutrition. The evidence shows that this is not the case and it may have been started by unscrupulous doctors and commercial health providers who are trying to sell nutritional supplements as treatments for ADHD.

It is recommended that all caregivers give the same amount of attention to their women's needs. This includes spending time with the child, providing positive reinforcement and making sure that they have healthy nutrition and a safe play environment. These are all necessary for good development in women.

It is also important for adults with ADHD to combine treatment with positive parenting which can help manage their symptoms.

A 2008 study investigated parents' perception of parents' own functioning, as well as effects on their women's behaviors and performance in school when no diagnosis of ADHD is made or a diagnosis of ADHD is not made. The researchers used a measure called Parental Report of Disruptive Behavior (PRDB). The PRDB measures frequency of disruptive behavior reported by both mother and father. From this, the researchers calculated a total severity score. The higher the total severity score, the more severe the symptoms were in each parent.

Having ADHD may mean some difficulties for your child later on in life, but with assistance and patience it can be managed and even turned into an advantage some times. In the end, it doesn't matter if they have ADHD or not; it matters how they live their life and what they do with what they are given. The goal is for them to be happy and successful. You just want them to grow up feeling fulfilled no matter what path they take in life.

Having a child with ADHD can be a challenge, but it can also be very rewarding. It's essential for both you and your child to understand what ADHD is and how best to deal with it. Understanding the signs of ADHD will help you understand your child, which will in turn help you deal with her more effectively.

ADHD is not a wonderful disorder that should be "treated" like diabetes or high blood pressure or killed off like the common cold. It doesn't matter if she outgrows her ADHD -- if she doesn't live as well without it as she could have, it means something was wrong with how you raised her.

Some people think having ADHD is a badge of honor. Others struggle with a feeling of personal failure. Here are some facts about the disorder that will give you more useful information to make good parenting decisions in the future:

Limitations of ADHD Sufferers

Unfortunately, many people don't know what to expect if they're diagnosed with ADHD. That's why we compiled this list of limitations for people who have been diagnosed with ADHD - as well as their loved ones - to understand them better.

- It's difficult for an individual to complete tasks that require reading a long-form text such as books or novels due to their lack of attention span.

- A person with ADHD tends to lose balance, which affects their ability to walk, run, and climb stairs.

- A person with ADHD often loses things such as keys, wallets, credit cards or glasses.

- That same individual can also misplace important documents such as bills or receipts. Addressed IEP Progress Reports (IDS) can be a good way to keep track of progress and help the teacher or parent know if goals are being met but they should not be your only way of keeping a record of progress.

- As adults, individuals with ADHD may be prone to alcohol and drug abuse because they are trying to self-medicate.

- For this same reason, it is common for people with ADHD to have problems keeping friendships and intimate relationships.

- Due to their lack of attention span, people with ADHD often suffer from short attention span. Reading or listening requires a lot of focus, so it's therefore not surprising if these individuals find it difficult to finish an entire article on the internet.

- Since it's common for people with ADHD to get distracted, they may have a problem following instructions or timelines. This can be frustrating for family members or co-workers. It is important to be patient and understand that the individual is not intentionally trying to be difficult, but rather struggling to stay focused.

- Individuals with ADHD are prone to mood swings, anxiety, and depression because they need consistency. If one topic is introduced and then something else starts instead, this can cause confusion in those with ADHD as they struggle to keep up.

- Those who have symptoms of ADHD on the behavior side also frequently have symptoms of it on the emotional side such as feeling restless, moody or easily frustrated.

- These individuals are often diagnosed with other disorders as well. Along with ADHD, it is not uncommon to be diagnosed with anxiety or depression, oppositional defiant disorder (ODD) or conduct disorder. It is a struggle for them to meet their potential if they live with so many limitations each day.

- The condition affects approximately 9-10% of school-aged women, and even more adults who struggle to get through their daily routines due to a lack of concentration and focus.

- It's no surprise why this is such a common condition; women today are busier and have so many distractions - from the TV, to video games, to cell phones - that it is difficult for them to pay attention in class or focus at any task. For those with ADHD, they are often unaware of their condition. Adults can get diagnosed with ADHD when one of their women receives the diagnosis.

- While this disease has many symptoms, there is no cure for it. The only thing that can be done to mitigate the disorder is to maintain a routine and setting up reminders. This can include alarms on a cell phone, Post-it notes and visual timetables. Another main point is to remember that you are not alone in this struggle.

Are you Inferior if You Have ADHD?

If you have ADHD, you're no different from anyone else. You might be able to multitask better than most people and have a refreshing perspective on life. No matter what your struggle is, there's something about ADHD that makes you who you are.

"Attention Deficit Hyperactivity Disorder" (ADHD) is a brain disorder that usually appears in childhood. It makes it hard for you to concentrate for long periods of time. Also, it makes it hard to control impulsive behavior. This means that you have trouble controlling your emotions, and you might get annoyed easily. It's also hard to sit still or pay attention for very long. All in all, ADHD makes it really hard to focus on one thing and finish a lot of tasks.

Besides having symptoms like these, ADHD can also cause many other problems like high-stress levels and sleeping problems. It's hard to handle all of this, but you are not alone. Most people with ADHD also feel very stressed about it, but there are ways to make your life easier.

Inattentive is when people don't pay attention and have a hard time focusing on anything for very long, and hyperactive-impulsive is when they're impulsive and have trouble controlling their movements or feelings.

It's hard to believe sometimes that people with ADHD can also be very smart. They might be really good at some things like programming, math, or sports. Most people with ADHD have very good memory skills, and they can think about things very quickly. You might know someone who has ADHD and they're very bright and enthusiastic.

There are also many strengths that come with having ADHD too. Many people with ADHD have a refreshing perspective on life; they live every day to the fullest and usually take every new situation as a gift. They are energetic, flexible, and active, a little bit like the energizer bunny in women's books. Many of them like sports or being around other people. They're usually very social and like to be around other people, or they do things that are fun and exciting. You might know someone who is very energetic or is always up for an adventure.

You also might know someone who is very artistic, creative, or has a good imagination. They can compliment others and have a good sense of humor. They might also have great intuition and become aware of situations before they happen. They can be great leaders too because they're motivated to help others get to where they want to go.

Of course, there are also some struggles with having ADHD too. Having ADHD means that you have to work really hard to control your behavior and pay attention in school. You might also have a hard time at home doing things around the house or paying attention when your mother is talking.

But there's nothing wrong with having ADHD. It's just like any other disorder or disability; it just makes it harder for you to focus on things. You can still be an amazing athlete or artist and do everything you want to do in life if you have the right help. "It can be very frustrating for people with ADHD, but they learn ways to cope and manage their condition." (Leahy) They become smarter by figuring out how they learn best and how they can handle their problems. They become stronger by knowing how to advocate for themselves and asking for help when they need it. They can be great leaders because they know what it's like to struggle and how to keep going.

Having ADHD doesn't mean that you're inferior. Just like anyone else, you can be just as successful in life no matter what your strengths or struggles are.

Adderall is one of the most common forms of ADHD stimulant drugs. Adderall helps children stay focused by making the body more efficient at completing tasks. This can result in improved ability to learn and remember information. Some people with ADHD may experience a very slight feeling of euphoria. However, this feeling typically wears off quickly and is not a desired effect by many people who take this drug for their condition.

Prescription stimulants are generally safe but they do have side effects that include headaches, stomachache, diarrhea, loss of appetite, upset stomach , changes in sleep patterns and depression . These side effects can be severe and severe side effects should be reported to your doctor.

Deficiencies in one or more of the following vitamins may cause or contribute to ADHD: vitamin B6 (pyridoxine) , vitamin B12 (cobalamin), chromium, and zinc . Deficiencies in these vitamins could result in your brain not functioning at its best.

If you are someone who has been prescribed stimulant drugs for ADHD, make sure you get plenty of exercise and healthy and nutritious foods. Make sure to use common sense when using your medications because there are other ways to help yourself out without the risk of dependence or other dangerous side effects.

Adderall belongs to a class of drugs known as stimulants. Many children struggle with this disorder so doctors prescribed them medications like Adderall to help them improve their ability to pay attention, learn new things, and focus on tasks they find challenging. But today there are many alternatives that can help people with ADHD.

ADHD is suspected in about one-third of American children but the number rises considerably among teenagers. A large number of kids born into wealthier families tend to receive this type of treatment. It is common for parents to diagnose their children not because they have any symptoms but because the child's behavior seems like it could be a disorder.

ADHD affects everybody differently and there is no single

cause for the condition. Many of these drugs are prescription, but you can find alternatives to Adderall. This will take you through some natural ways to help your child with ADHD.

Children who have ADHD often struggle with depressive symptoms or even worse suicidal thoughts. They tend to have low self-esteem and related problems that could be helped by the use of herbs like St. John's wort, valerian root , kava kava , ashwagandha , and other options. Stimulant drugs can cause other types of side effects, including depression, so these alternatives should always be considered before resorting to other drugs.

The following herbs have been studied extensively and found to have a calming effect in people with ADHD:

1. Chamomile: This herb calms the nervous system, so it could be a good choice for someone with ADHD.

2. Passionflower : This herb is used in Chinese medicine to calm the nervous system and it can be taken as a gel or as a supplement in capsule form.

3. Preliminary research shows that ginkgo Biloba is an effective herbal treatment for ADHD symptoms when taken at doses of 60-120 mg per day for up to six weeks.

4. In a study of 112 people with ADHD, taking Ginkgo biloba for 12 weeks was associated with significant symptom improvement.

5. St. John's Wort : Another herb that can be taken as a cream or gel to help reduce depressive symptoms caused by the stimulant drugs used to treat ADHD. It also can be taken as a supplement in capsule form.

6. Valerian root : This herb is good for treating anxiety and is used to promote restful sleep . You should start with small doses because it can cause drowsiness and sedation in high amounts.

7. Ashwagandha : This herb can be taken in capsule form or tea. Its calming effect helps the nervous system reduce jitteriness, common in ADHD.

8. Kava kava : Some studies have shown that Kava kava can help reduce anxiety for people who have ADHD.

9. Although it has many side effects, the important thing to note is that this herb is well-studied and has been used without much risk of side effects to treat ADHD for hundreds of years Ayurveda .

It turns out that these herbs are not only safe but very effective.

These are some herbs that can help you or your child with ADHD. Make sure that you talk to your doctor first before you start taking any supplements because some herbs should not be taken together. You may want to try them first without trying other medications.

The pathology of ADHD has been widely studied and documented. The disorder is characterized by an inattention and hyperactivity-impulsivity. Symptoms of both inattention and hyperactivity-impulsivity can be present from early childhood, with symptom onset during primary school.

The American Psychiatric Association (APA) decided in 2013 to revise their diagnostic criteria for ADHD. The revised criteria identified that the core symptoms of ADHD include problems staying focused on tasks, difficulty organizing tasks and activities, and excessive distraction both during the task and without. The new ICD-11 includes two main categories of disorder: "ADHD" and "Hyperkinetic Disorder". Certified physicians are allowed to diagnose both disorders so long as they are used correctly in conjunction with patient history.

The medical community has long recognized the symptoms, but there is no consensus on possible causes. Theories explaining the development of ADHD include genetics, brain injuries during birth or in early childhood, family dysfunction during parenting, infections and diet. Despite a lack of conclusive data for its cause, there is a wide range of evidence that points to a variety of both psychological and biological factors.

The ADHD community is more likely to suffer from a learning disability than the general population. This is most likely due to an inconsistency with the way in which the brains of those affected by ADHD function and an inconsistency with how juvenile justice systems punish adolescents with ADHD.

Genetic factors account for 67–77% of variation in severity in symptoms in children with ADHD. This is true of all disorders, including schizophrenia, bipolar disorder and depression. A study analyzing the characteristics of children with ADHD found that their symptom profile could be predicted by factors such as their family history of ADHD, aggressive behavior in childhood, response to stimulants and DNA polymorphisms. Other genetic studies have demonstrated no correlation between DNA sequence polymorphisms in genes for dopamine transporters or other genes known to affect dopamine function and ADHD symptoms.

Clinical features are the main markers used when diagnosing ADHD today. The symptoms are also known as "attentional deficit hyperactivity disorder" or simply AD/HD. This term is a somewhat recent one, and a more accurate name would be "attentional deficit disorder with hyperactivity". Physicians prefer this newer term because it encompasses the symptoms of inattention and hyperactivity better.

In most situations, the exact etiology of this complication is unknown.

It is believed that 75% of the risk originates from genetic factors. Certain environmental hazards, such as toxins and infections, can lead to brain damage and birth defects. It appears that the association isn't based on parenting or disciplining approach.

It impacts anywhere between 5 and 7 percent of children when diagnosed using DSM-IV criteria, and little over 1 percent of children diagnosed with the use of ICD-10 criteria. A global study concluded that 84.7 million individuals are suffering from the illness in 2019. It seems to change depending on diagnosis, with national differences comparable.

It is thought that girls with ADHD are less commonly identified, because their symptoms tend to be subtler than boys', and their symptoms are sometimes misdiagnosed.

About 50% of children diagnosed with ADHD grow up to continue having symptoms, whereas 2-5% of adults have it. For adults, inner restlessness is a distinct possibility rather than a hyperactive state.

Compensatory coping mechanisms are commonly employed by adults as a means of compensating for their disabilities. It can be difficult to identify because it's indistinguishable from other diseases, as well as typical behavior.ADHD management in each country may be different, and often entails some mix of treatments, including counseling, medicines, and lifestyle modifications.

According to the British standard, the first line of treatment is an environmental change including education for the patient and those assisting them about ADHD.

If symptoms continue to be present, the three options given are parent training, medications, or psychotherapy, notably cognitive behavioral therapy, all dependent on age. In Canada and the U.S., recommendations state that both pharmacological and behavioral interventions should be used simultaneously to treat children, except for those who are aged 3 or younger.

The only treatment option in these cases is behavioral therapy.

Some kids may have side effects that can be dangerous, but at least the treatments are good for a year and a half, unless they have some major adverse effect. There has been much debate regarding ADHD, its diagnosis, and treatment during the last three decades.

Controversies are occurring and include professionals including doctors, teachers, legislators, parents, and the media. Topics include the treatment of ADHD, including the causes of ADHD and the usage of stimulant medicines.

A consensus among healthcare practitioners is that ADHD is a legitimate diagnosis in both children and adults, and scientific discourse is only over diagnosing and treating the disorder. The diagnosis of ADD used to be referred to as "hyperkinetic response of children" before 1980, and it became formally called ADD in 1987. Symptoms of ADHD were first recorded in the medical literature in the 18th century.

These issues are often thought of as "bad behaviors" but they are actually part of an individual's neurological development.

Why Does ADHD Happen?

ADHD people must understand that their condition will not disappear on its own. ADHD happens due to anatomical and developmental issues in the brain. The brain development of people with ADHD takes longer than other people. ADHD is caused by too much or not enough dopamine in the brain. It is important to treat ADHD. ADHD is not a bad thing; it is actually a symptom (ADHD).

It is not known why it happens. It is thought that it is caused by genetics, during the embryo development in the mother's body. For example, the head is growing at the speed of the body. Environmental factors further complicate these development issues. For example, there are many studies that have shown that children of people suffering from ADHD tend to have more problems at school than children of people without ADHD. ADHD cannot be cured immediately. It can be treated, but not cured. If you have ADHD, you will have it for the rest of your life. If you have suboptimal attention, you have suboptimal attention, but you can live a normal, productive, healthy life.

Different Types of ADHD

One of the most common reasons for seeking an ADHD assessment is to find out what type of ADHD you may have. This book will talk about all the different types of ADHD in adults.

1) Primarily Inattentive Type: People with this type are easily distracted and forgetful, but they're otherwise good at paying attention to things that interest them. They also have trouble organizing tasks or activities, or finishing work on time.

2) Primarily Hyperactive Type: A person with this type has a hard time sitting still and often fidgets throughout the day. They constantly feel restless, and may get up frequently to walk around.

3) Combined Type: People with this type of ADHD have symptoms of both the inattentive type and the hyperactive-impulsive type. They tend to be fidgety and unable to concentrate, and they also tend to be extremely impatient.

4) Secondary ADHD: This kind of ADHD only occurs as a result of problems with other mental health conditions or traumatic brain injuries, or from substance abuse. If you have secondary ADHD, you'll most likely have other symptoms associated with your condition (like self-harm or hallucinations), which are different than the symptoms associated with typical adult ADHD.

5) Mixed Type: This is a combination of both the inattentive

and hyperactive-impulsive subtypes. People with this type tend to struggle with their attention, easily distracted, and will often have trouble paying attention to their surroundings. However, they are very active and energetic, and often act out when they're in class.

6) Overlearning Mix Type: People with this type of ADHD think "over-hard" or excessive amounts of things. They'll often do things over and over again until they're completed correctly or even painfully correct, but not necessarily in a positive way.

7) Not Otherwise Specified (NOS) Type: Basically, this type of ADHD is a variation of any of the above types. Like mixed type, it's a combination of both inattentive and hyperactive-impulsive. However, it's not enough to be diagnosed as a different subtype, so you'll be diagnosed with NOS.

8) Attention deficit disorder without hyperactivity (ADHD-WO): This type is rare and only occurs in older school-age children and adults with symptoms like ADHD but without hyperactivity. It's also sometimes referred to as "pure ADHA" or "atypical presentation.

9) Unspecified ADHD: When someone has symptoms of adult ADHD and the doctor can't figure out what type of ADHD they have, it's called unspecified adult ADHD. This is pretty uncommon, but if you're receiving treatment for your adult ADHD and still aren't getting better, you will likely be diagnosed with this type.

10) Other Specified Attention-Deficit/Hyperactivity Disorder (ADHD)-NOS: Like specified above, this type of attention deficit disorder is a variation on any of the above types. However, it's not enough to be diagnosed as another subtype or NOS.

11) Mixed Type with other specified: Some ADHD experts believe that people with this type have a combo of both inattentive and hyperactive-impulsive symptoms.

12) Mixed Type with unspecified: Just like mixed type, this is a combination of both inattentive and hyperactive-impulsive symptoms. However, it's not enough to be diagnosed as a subtype or NOS.

13) Borderline Personality Disorder: BPD is a mental disorder characterized by a lot of distressing emotions, such as feeling like you're not good enough or that you're a failure. People with this condition are also often haunted by recurrent thoughts of death, engaging in high-risk behaviors, and having bouts of uncontrollable anger, depression, or anxiety. These symptoms are different than those displayed with ADHD in adults. If a person who has ADHD also has a borderline personality disorder, it'll most likely be the secondary type. BPD on the other hand is commonly seen in people with ADHD as well as with substance abuse issues and/or anxiety disorders.

14) Bipolar Disorder: If a person has bipolar disorder, they are constantly up and down in mood, or even experience lots of swings back and forth between depression and mania. However, if a person with ADHD also has this disorder, it's called the combined type.

Chapter 2:   Characteristic of ADHD

There are some people who have symptoms from both categories while there are others who face only one of them. In this part, we are going to talk about the characteristics of ADHD in detail. But remember that you are not to use the information mentioned in this part for performing self-diagnosis. You can, however, refer to the information in order to figure out for certain whether your problem needs special attention or not. Once you visit a specialist, he/she will be able to diagnose the problem to be ADHD or something else.

Distractibility and Difficulty to Concentrate

Distractibility will, no doubt, be one of the biggest barriers in your path when you are trying to deal with ADHD. But first, let us explore what the term "distractibility" truly means. It means that you don't have the ability to steer clear of visual distractions or any other unimportant distractions and do the task that you have been assigned. For example, there are several adults with ADHD who simply cannot work when there is the slightest noise in their surroundings—it can be something as simple as someone's footsteps. In short, when people have ADHD, they sort of do not know how to filter out the distractions. So, when there are too many things happening in their surroundings, all of that automatically starts competing for her attention.

When a person with ADHD experiences this feeling of distractibility, they cannot usually frame it in words. This is mainly because they themselves do not understand it that well. People often see them as space cadets or airheads. In fact, when ADHD goes unnoticed or undiagnosed until adulthood, people who struggle with distractibility often think that they are scatterbrained and that it cannot possibly be a part of any disorder. That is why it is so vital that you address the problem of distractibility separately in your treatment plan because it is definitely one of the most overwhelming parts of suffering from ADHD.

Impulsivity

Impulsivity is one of those symptoms of ADHD that people often ignore. Being impulsive doesn't only mean that the person has zero sense of self-discipline or is rude. Impulsiveness comes from changes in the brain's signaling system, which is impacted in a person with ADHD. So, a person takes random actions without thinking it through. They completely overlook the consequences that their actions are going to have.

They simply act on a whim. So, an adult with ADHD might answer people rudely all of a sudden or scream because they are angry.

Hyperactivity

The characteristics of hyperactivity are more commonly noticed in children than in adults. Even when it comes to adults, you will find that it is men who display this symptom more than women. This symptom refers to the behavior of constant fidgeting and the need to move. Some people have the habit of shuffling their feet or continuously tapping their fingers even while they are in the middle of a conversation. There are different ways in which the symptom of hyperactivity can manifest itself. But you have to remember that when people grow old, hyperactivity is the first symptom that dies down, and so, you cannot identify or diagnose ADHD solely based on hyperactivity. In any case, if someone is suffering from a problem of hyperactivity, they will not be able to sit in a single place for a long time. They will also not prefer doing quiet activities and have a knack for energetic activities.

Exaggerated Emotions

Emotions are often heightened in adults who have ADHD. The root cause of this characteristic also lies in the brain. Adult ADHD often causes people to get flooded by a certain emotion all of a sudden, even though that emotion was only momentary. This is mainly because of some problems in the working memory. Unfortunately, the system of diagnosis, which is currently followed for ADHD, doesn't focus on exaggerated emotions or emotional challenges. But if we are to follow the research-based evidence, then we'll see, then it is shown that people with ADHD have a hot temper, impatience, a very low tolerance level to frustration and excitability.

These challenges that we are talking about also find their origin in the human brain. In usual scenarios, anyone who has ADHD won't seem that much affected by someone's feelings or actions and would appear to be completely unaware. But there are times when these emotions become exaggerated because of impairments. Our emotions are relayed through various signals in the brain, and in people with ADHD, these networks do not function the way they should and are somewhat limited.

So, if something is denied to the adult, they often get filled with rage and cannot keep their anger under control even when the issue is not that important. Thus, they end up giving an extreme response to something very insignificant. This phenomenon is also known as flooding because the emotion at that point in time has taken up all the space inside his/her head. It is very similar to a virus attack on your laptop, where the laptop does not function properly because the virus takes up the entire hard disk. So, the person starts focusing on that one single emotion and overlooks everything else. They cannot take in any information that is given to them at that moment.

Every action that we take in our lives is motivated by our emotions. So, when ADHD is either not diagnosed or not treated properly in adults, they often seek immediate gratification, and for this, they pursue only those activities that can give them that. That is why, in the long term, they fail to provide a consistent effort to those tasks whose rewards are going to be realized at a later time. Moreover, there have been several brain imaging studies done on ADHD patients that show that the ADHD brain does not identify satisfaction or pleasure like that of a normal brain, especially for tasks whose rewards are delayed.

Common Signs and Symptoms You Need to Know

Everyone has ADHD sometimes. It doesn't mean someone is a bad person or that they're lazy. There are just certain symptoms that people with ADHD may display and these symptoms can definitely cause problems in their lives and relationships. If you're struggling with something like anxiety, impulsivity, or disorganization then you might have an issue with ADHD too.

So what do we know about symptoms of ADHD? Well, according to Psychology Today it's defined as "a neurodevelopmental disorder (NLD) characterized by development-related problems such as difficulty sustaining attention, hyperactivity/impulsivity and difficulty controlling emotions." It affects about 10% of the general population -- around 18 million people in the US alone. When it comes to the ways these symptoms affect someone, ADHD is divided into three subtypes.

According to listservs, here are some distinct symptoms of each subtype:

ADHD-PI : No longer than average attention span, impulsive behavior that leads to poor decisions.

ADHD-S : Similar to PI but with an explosive temper and more serious mismanagement of anger. It causes more negative relationships with others than positive ones.

ADHD-SX: Has all of the above + excessive hyperactivity and impulsive behavior that impairs functioning in settings demanding sustained attention or where there is a need for emotional control or social skills.

So, what do these symptoms look like in real life? In a nutshell, people with ADHD may find it difficult to complete tasks they've been given. They might have difficulty paying attention when things don't go their way. They might experience anger issues with little provocation. They might be "easily distracted" -- meaning that if they're in a situation where they need to pay attention or focus properly, then they do a poor job of it. All of this leads to more problems completing tasks and achieving goals.

ADHD also affects the way people deal with stress. When they are stressed or under pressure, their behavior tends to escalate to the point where they do things that aren't good for themselves or others. One study even found that adults with ADHD had a greater number of borderline personality disorders than the general population.

If you are struggling with any of the following symptoms, it is likely that you have ADHD.

• Strong sense of self-identity

• Fidgeting behavior or impulsivity, especially in the classroom or workplace

- Easily bored and seeking activities that stimulate interest

- Difficulty remaining attentive (can't seem to pay attention for more than two consecutive minutes)

- Impulsiveness (e.g. blurting out answers in school, interrupting a conversation, or blurting out ideas at the dinner table)

- Trouble waiting their turn

- Often talk too much

- Difficulties with paying attention and following through with instructions and directions

- Difficulty starting tasks, making decisions, or finishing tasks

- Engaging in multiple conversations at once (e.g. text messaging while listening to a speaker).

- Having a short attention span and flitting from one subject to another, one activity to another.

- Blurting out comments or answers in class, rushing through homework assignments, not completing projects or chores.

- Lack of organization (e.g. making careless mistakes while preparing for assignments, leaving things undone at home or work, or forgetting to bring something with them when they leave their room)

- Difficulty keeping a schedule and following through on tasks (e.g. skipping breakfast, missing appointments)

- Repeating routines until they are perfect (e.g., playing catch-up after being behind on homework; getting dressed and ready for school several times each day; needing to do homework over and over until it is complete)

- Having difficulty organizing their thoughts and direction (e.g. not knowing what to say in a conversation, not being able to recall information they learned in the past, and difficulty making decisions)

• Having a difficult time shifting from one activity to another (e.g. From homework you go straight to dinner and then jump right into sports practice)

• Having trouble relaxing (e.g. working out or doing homework until the wee morning hours)

• Frequently losing their way or forgetting daily routines.

• Getting so deeply involved with an activity that it can interfere with their health, appetite, sleep, or regular daily activities (e.g. working out, reading, playing video/computer games, or watching TV)

• Being embarrassed or reluctant to sit still when required by a classroom teacher

• Having trouble keeping their balance while sitting or standing (e.g. they are often bumping into things or running into people)

• Getting more restless and unable to concentrate when they are required to stay still for a period of time (e.g. during a movie)

• Acting without thinking (e.g., buying something without considering the consequences; starting conversations without thinking about what they might say; approaching dangerous situations without considering the consequence; jumping from one activity to another and never finishing anything).

• Speaking before thinking (e.g., sharing too much information; blurting out something negative about someone or a group of people)

• Lacking empathy for others

• Frequently being ridiculed, teased, or bullied by peers

• Having difficulty describing or putting words to their

feelings, often mistaking their feelings for someone else's

• Acting before they think (e.g., rushing into dangerous situations without considering the consequences).

If you have a hyperactive or inattentive type of ADHD, this could be a list for you!

. Remember that ADD/ADHD is not just one disorder but many different disorders.

Common symptoms of ADHD

-Inability to focus on one task at a time, jumping from subject to subject

-Hyperactivity and impulsiveness which can lead to problems with self-control and self-esteem

-Difficulty staying organized; struggles with time management

-Poor decision-making; tends towards impulsive actions which can lead to wrong decisions. This includes not following through with plans, failing to complete tasks appropriately (such as chores) or failing school work (not turning in assignments).

-Disregard for rules and authority

-Difficulty following multi-step directions, difficulty "listening to" or processing what is being said

-Inferiority complex; feels different from others, believes that no one understands him/her

-Low self-esteem and a sense of being a failure

-Poor memory; difficulty remembering things just learned or things that have been asked previously. The trouble with retention/recall of dates and timeframes. Difficulty memorizing information presented in lectures. Inability to remember names of people met for the first time as well as friends and acquaintances. Tendency to misplace things.

-Impatience; feeling that things are taking too long

-Bad temper, easily provoked to anger

-Frequent mood swings/moodiness, emotionally sensitive. Can have periods of being high or down for no apparent reason

-Talkative more than others of same age group; more hyper, restless activity than others of same age group. May be perceived by teachers as "sloppy", "careless", "unfocused", "hyper" or "distractible". They may be perceived by peers as being "bored easily" or having a short attention span.

Most people with ADD/ADHD have several symptoms of the above.

The main characteristics of ADHD are:

-Problems in concentration; difficulty in remaining focused on one task. Often can't maintain attention on what needs to be done. Frequently interrupted by distractions that the person with ADD/ADHD doesn't even notice. They can't seem to get other things out of the way so they can get to what needs to be done (they don't appear to do it intentionally).

-Impulsivity; characterized by acting before thinking; may act on impulse, without seeming concern for consequences. Can have problems with self-control which leads to problems with self-esteem.

-Hyperactivity, is characterized by excessive restlessness or excessive levels of activity which often seems inappropriate. Can have problems with self-control which leads to problems with self-esteem.

-Carelessness, is characterized by a lack of attention to detail or failure to complete tasks. Often fail to follow through on assignments or chores. There is often an appearance of being messy or untidy.

-Disorganisation, characterized by difficulty in organizing tasks and activities; can make it difficult to get started on tasks requiring organization, excessive procrastination. Difficulty keeping track of personal belongings; may frequently misplace things or be confused about where they have put them after using them. Difficulty keeping track of time; frequent tardiness and frequently late for appointments and deadlines. Can often forget what has already been accomplished. Frequently changes plans and fails to follow through on previous plans.

-Withdrawal, is characterized by a lack of energy and focus on tasks. May feel bored easily, unmotivated, drowsy, listless. Characterized by a feeling of "not being me"; can appear depressed or sad

-Hyperfocus, characterized by having immersive attention focused on one thing at a time which appears to distract from other things that need to be done. May feel as if they can't get their mind on track with the activities of daily life because they are too interested in what is going on at this one thing or activity or project they are involved with at the moment.

People who suffer from ADHD (particularly those with the inattentive subtype) may have difficulty describing what they are feeling. As children this means that they do not know how to describe their problems to an adult who will listen. As adults, it means that they do not know how to verbalize what is going on inside of them.

Many people report that they feel "disconnected", "disoriented", "disconnected", "dissociated", or "spaced out". They feel as though things are "not real" or are being experienced through a haze or fog so that the world doesn't even seem real. This can cause problems with depression, anxiety, isolation or loneliness.

People with ADHD (particularly those with the inattentive subtype) may feel like they don't know who they are, or that they are losing touch with themselves. They can feel "tired" or "not awake", they can feel like "I'm not myself", "I'm not real", or "who is this?". Sometimes people can feel like their feelings (or part of themselves) is missing, like something has been taken away from them. This can lead to depression, anxiety, isolation or loneliness.

Those with ADHD (particularly those without hyperactivity) often report feeling bored easily, even when something seems very interesting on the surface. They may be unmotivated to do anything or feel like they are "sluggish" or "not moving" at all.

Those with ADHD report feeling anxious. Most people with ADHD report intense feelings of anxiety about personal failures, but also intense feelings of anxiety about relationships, health, sexual problems and school work. This can cause problems with depression, anxiety, isolation or loneliness.

People have different ways that they cope with their symptoms of hyperactivity or inattention. For some it means being "on the go". For others it means being "hyper vigilant". Other people cope by being "methodical". Others cope by being "perfectionistic". These coping strategies help people to manage their symptoms of hyperactivity or inattention, but they also cause problems. They can cause problems with self-esteem and self-image, and can lead to depression and anxiety.

The most common classifications of attention deficit hyperactivity disorder (ADHD) are:

Hyperactivity is not required for the diagnosis of ADHD; however only those with the combined type meet criteria for both disorders. Often those with the predominantly inattentive presentation were not diagnosed as children as their hyperactivity was more subtle (they were often called "dreamers" or called "the still small voice"). This can lead to a huge sense of relief when people are finally diagnosed with

ADHD at the adult age.

People who suffer from ADHD tend to have a decreased negative response to a stimulant-type drug, such as Ritalin or Adderall. This means that after taking a stimulant-type drug, people with ADHD experience their symptoms much less severely. They tend to be much more alert and focused.

In the past, when it was believed that people could not learn while they were taking Ritalin or Adderall, many experiences of adults showing symptoms of ADHD only when they were on drugs were attributed to "speed freaks" and "amphetamine abusers". This is not true, and only about 1% of those taking Ritalin or Adderall will exhibit symptoms of ADHD when they first start taking them. This strongly suggests that the drug has no negative effects other than the stimulant-type boost it gives to many people who are not affected by ADHD.

Many people find it helpful to understand the symptoms of ADHD in relation to their own experiences and feelings. Because ADHD symptoms can mimic other physical and mental conditions, such as depression, anxiety and stress, it may be difficult for some people with ADHD to distinguish whether their symptoms are caused by something "real" or whether they are caused by something "all in their head". It is common for people with ADHD to have a long history of being told that their problems are "just in their head", and it takes a lot of courage and determination for them to persistently pursue a diagnosis. Once diagnosed, many adults feel relieved.

In order to make these distinctions, people need to be able to describe their symptoms, to distinguish different types of symptoms from one another, and learn how these symptoms cause problems for themselves or for others. This can be hard work because it requires that people understand why they think or feel the way that they do. This can be very difficult because most people with ADHD do not readily understand how their brain operates, let alone why they have the particular issues that they have.

Many people understand their own descriptions of their experience better if they are able to draw it out on paper. Drawing pictures of what you are experiencing in relation to your own life helps you to see things that you may not be able to see or articulate when looking at words on a page. It helps you to visualise the problems you are facing, and this can help you find solutions.

An alternative way of understanding your experience is by using collages, metaphors or symbols. Such non-verbal means of expression can be very effective for people who have a hard time getting their feelings or thoughts written down. Once they have been drawn or written, they can be put in a place where you will see them regularly so that you can get feedback from others about how these ideas reflect on your experience of being ADHD.

A third way to get a dialogue going is to talk with a group of friends or a group that shares your concern about ADHD.

Many people find that one-to-one counselling is the most helpful way of helping to understand their difficulties. Counselling helps people to take accountability for their behaviours, learn new coping strategies and figure out what causes them problems. It encourages people to learn more about themselves so that they can be more effective in school or work, improve their relationships with others and meet the challenges of living independently.

A major problem that many adults face with ADHD is having difficulty getting along with other adults who also have ADHD. Adults with ADHD often feel "different" from other adults, and this can lead to grief, shame and embarrassment. This can be very difficult for adults because it tends to be a source of conflict in the social world.

In order to understand how these conflicts can arise, people need to understand that their ADHD does not make them any less aware or intelligent than other people. In fact it is much more likely that people who have ADHD are more aware and intelligent than most other people around them, but they often do not know this because they do not have a way of expressing what they know in a way that others will understand.

Many people with ADHD also suffer from depression, anxiety, substance abuse, personality disorders and domestic violence problems. This is because life is difficult for many people who have ADHD. They often feel different from other people so they can feel isolated and lonely.

People with ADHD are often very impulsive and can be easily provoked into acting or speaking before considering the consequences of their actions or words. This often leads to problems in romantic relationships where partners become frustrated by what they see as a continual lack of consideration for their feelings or needs. Likewise, people with ADHD are often perceived as being "lazy" because they have trouble sticking with projects for a long time, but they may not understand that they are easily distracted by their own interests.

It can be hard for some people who have ADHD to live independently. They may have problems holding down jobs because they are easily distracted. This can lead to frustration, anger and depression. Many people are able to use their creative talents at work or school in order to make up for their difficulty staying on tasks that demand concentration or persistence. Even so, many adults with ADHD are more likely to be fired or otherwise given the boot from their job than are most people who have not been diagnosed.

This is because employers often have preconceptions of what an adult with ADHD "should" look like. They tend to think of adults with ADHD as being someone who is irresponsible,

irresponsible, lazy and irresponsible.

Adults with ADHD also often struggle with issues of intimacy, as they tend to be more easily distracted and impulsive than most people.

The first step that many adults who have ADHD take in order to overcome their difficulties is the creation of an "ADHD self-help group" where they can gather together with others who share interests and understandings of their experience of having ADHD. An Adult ADHD Self-help Group is a social networking group of individuals who share similar experiences, beliefs and interests. It is a place where adults with ADHD can learn from each other within a supportive and non-judgmental environment.

In Adult ADHD Self-help Groups, adults with ADHD meet regularly to discuss the challenges that they face as individuals who also have ADHD. They also share their ideas about how to cope with these challenges, and find ways of working together in order to form community that provides mutual support and understanding.

ADHD groups can be very supportive for people who are members of them because they provide belonging for people who may be isolated due to the nature of their condition. They are also an effective way for adults with ADHD to seek advice from others who share their experiences, because they are trained to give non-judgmental support and understanding.

Adult ADHD Self-help Groups often offer educational experiences as well as the opportunity to find common ground with others who have similar problems. As well, people can use these groups as a way to help them learn about what they can do within the context of living with ADHD. Many people find that these groups are an effective solution for many of their social issues related to having ADHD.

ADHD coaching is a collaborative relationship between the

coach and the client centered around specific goals which arise out of their unique situations. ADHD coaching strives to set up a collaborative relationship in order to improve clients' skill sets in areas related to ADHD. ADHD coaching aims at improving quality of life and self-esteem, and establishing personal goals for bettering the client's life with ADHD.

ADHD coaching involves a critical goal-setting process with frequent feedback. The goals which are set out by the client are developed in collaboration with the coach who will give feedback on how well he/she is achieving them. The coach also provides positive reinforcement and feedback on the client's progress and achievements. The coach and client remain in a constant dialogue about how they are doing in order to help them reach their goals.

ADHD Coaching is not a temporary, stand-around type of intervention. ADHD Coaching aims at achieving specific, measurable objectives related to the client's situation. Adherence to such goals is monitored and updated by the coach regularly. The coach will be involved in helping the client reach these goals in order for him/her to improve quality of life and self-esteem, establish personal goals for bettering their life with ADHD, and achieve personalized solutions that address their unique situations.

In order for ADHD coaching to be successful, it is important that the coach and client have a good rapport in a comfortable and safe environment. ADHD coaching is a collaborative process which requires trust in both parties. It is best when both parties can meet in person in order to establish this trust.

With all of the information in the world about ADHD, it's important to understand that it's not something that people are born with.

ADHD Diagnosis in Adults

ADHD is something that many people are familiar with. It may bring to mind children who have difficulty paying attention and children who are energetic or impulsive. Adults, on the other hand, are seldom diagnosed with or treated for it.

Who is at risk for adult ADHD? Every person who has ADHD has the condition as a kid. Some people might get diagnosed and are aware of it. On the other hand, some were not diagnosed early and they learn about it later in life. While many children with ADHD get cured of the condition, about 60% of adults continue to suffer. Adult attention deficit hyperactivity disorder (ADHD) appears to affect both genders equally. There is currently no treatment for ADHD.

A combination of sustained difficulties, such as trouble in paying attention, impulsive conduct and hyperactivity, is characterized by ADHD. Adult attention deficit hyperactivity disorder may result in unstable relationships, poor performance in job or school, very low self-esteem and many other issues. Even though it is referred regarded as adult ADHD, indications begin in early infancy and last throughout maturity. ADHD is not often noticed or is diagnosed until someone is an adult, as it happens in many other instances. The symptoms of this disorder in adults might not be as obvious as those symptoms in children, but they are still there. Adults may see a reduction in impulsivity, although they may continue to battle with hyperactivity, restlessness and trouble in paying attention.

The therapy of adult ADHD is quite similar to the treatment of pediatric ADHD. The treatment of Adult ADHD involves medication, psychological counseling, psychotherapy and treatment for many other co-occurring mental health disorders such as bipolar disorder.

If a person has adult attention deficit disorder, he may find it difficult to do the following:

- Comply with all instructions.

- Keep the information in mind.

- Concentrate.

- Make a plan for your tasks.

- Complete his job on time.

These symptoms may vary in severity from moderate to severe, and they can alter over time. They may create problems in various settings, including the family, the workplace and school. Getting therapy for ADHD and learning how to manage the condition may be beneficial. The majority of individuals learn to adapt to the circumstances. In addition, individuals with ADHD may discover their unique talents and achieve success.

Effects of Adult ADHD

It is estimated that over 7.8 million adult Americans have Attention Deficit Hyperactivity Disorder (ADHD). ADHD is a neurological disorder that affects the way one thinks, acts and feels. There are many symptoms of ADHD, but some common signs include poor time management, inattention, impulsivity and difficulty sustaining focus on tasks. While adults with ADHD often struggle to complete tasks and maintain regular schedules from day to day; the most pernicious impact of the disorder on adults is their inability to develop intimate relationships. In addition to these challenges are trying financial issues as well as other challenges related such as depression or anxiety disorders for those afflicted with this condition. It is estimated that individuals with ADHD make up 7% of the population, yet they account for roughly 25% of the diagnosed cases of depression in adults. The cost of diagnosing and treating adult ADHD is reportedly over $11 billion each year.

Within this article, I will review some of the health and

economic pitfalls adults with ADHD can face. This book will also consider the limitations surrounding drug medications for adults with ADHD as well as alternative methods for treatment.

Effects on Mental Health:

In many cases, adults with ADHD are often described as possessing a childlike demeanor which results in poor personal or social skills when compared to their peers or past experiences. Many adults with ADHD placed in positions of authority are criticized for the inability to meet deadlines or delegate tasks, thus creating an atmosphere of distrust between workers, supervisors and employers.

People with ADHD often experience low self-esteem and depression from the constant internal struggle regarding emotional regulation. Adults with ADHD are more likely to self-medicate with alcohol or drugs as well as experience high rates of divorce. There is a strong correlation between men with ADHD and criminal convictions for violent offenses such as homicide or manslaughter.

Anxiety Disorders and Adult ADHD

Research has shown that adults who have been diagnosed with an anxiety disorder often have a higher likelihood of being diagnosed with ADHD. Adults with ADHD who suffer from severe symptoms of depression are also likely to exhibit some of the symptoms associated with anxiety disorders such as panic attacks, phobias and obsessive fears.

Exacerbating the Issues: The Relationship

The inability to properly manage relationships is often a sign that ADHD is at play within an adult's life. A lack of social skills can cause awkward exchanges on dates or in public for those with this condition leading to miscommunications and misunderstanding. Because many adults struggle with expressing their thoughts and feelings in a forthright manner, there may be misunderstandings between friends or family members over what is actually being communicated. Some adults with ADHD are able to fully express themselves in a way that others might perceive as disruptive, insensitive or immature.

Negative Consequences: Employment

There are several disadvantages in the employment realm for those with ADHD. Many employers will not hire workers who have been diagnosed with ADHD, which can lead to a high unemployment rate. The inability to complete tasks and meet deadlines is often a detriment to the employment of adults with ADHD. There are also many people who are undiagnosed or unwilling to accept ADHD as a problem, fearing the stigma associated with it.

Drug Interactions

Risk of drug interactions can be increased when using amphetamines and methylphenidate concurrently. These medications are commonly prescribed for those who exhibit symptoms of hyperactivity in children, but can cause adverse effects if used by adults. Adults who take methylphenidate can experience racing thoughts and a decrease in motor skills. Adverse side effects associated with taking amphetamines include an increased risk of alcohol or drug use and a decrease in motor skills. Some of the most common side effects of treatment are insomnia, headache, nausea, stomach-aches and vomiting. Concerns exist that amphetamines can increase the risk of psychosis, anxiety disorders or depression within those who already suffer from these conditions.

Alternatives to Medication

There are many alternative methods for treating ADHD that do not involve medication. How to Stop Worrying and Start Living is one of the most commonly used books on this subject matter as well as books by Martha Beck and Dr. Wayne Dyer. There are also self-help groups for adults with ADHD including ones run by the American Attention Deficit Disorders Association (ADDA). In addition, adults with ADHD can find effective treatments that offer alternatives to medication through the use of occupational therapy, neurofeedback, special diets and lifestyle changes.

There are many factors that can contribute to the development of ADHD in a person including genetics, prenatal environment or complications at birth, drug use during pregnancy, as well as other environmental factors such as diet and stress. While there is no cure for ADHD in adults, there are many treatments available that can be helpful to those who suffer from this condition.

Attention deficit hyperactivity disorder (ADHD) is a neurobehavioral disorder of children that also affects inattentive, hyperactive and impulsive symptoms in adults. It is estimated that 3 to 5 percent of children have ADHD with an additional 3 to 5 percent being undiagnosed. The condition can be genetic or it can be caused by some other factor such as illness or injury. Many experts believe that the condition stems from a disruption in the levels of dopamine or norepinephrine within the brain, which can cause a host of behavioral problems.

Researchers have noted that many people who are diagnosed with ADHD marry and divorce more often than their peers without this disorder. There are many misconceptions about children and adults with ADHD and the disorder, which can lead to social isolation. Many people have become concerned about treating ADHD in children with medication, which is not recommended for use before the age of 6 years old due to possible side effects. The concerns about using drugs for ADHD in children has made many parents concerned about exposing their child to the dangers of taking these medications.

There are a number of treatments that can be used for adults diagnosed with ADHD. In some cases, individuals will still need a combination of these treatment options as there are some comorbid issues that can occur as well as fitness in some cases. Depending on the severity of the disorder, a number of adults with ADHD can find themselves incarcerated for violent offenses. While there are treatments available, adults are often reluctant to seek help due to fear of stigma associated with ADHD and the treatment options available.

Chapter 3: Executive Functioning: How it Can Help You

Executive functioning is a huge concept that includes a variety of behaviors. You may have heard it called "executive skills," "executive attention," or "mental flexibility."

In this article, we'll be focusing on the aspect of executive functioning that helps you with task management, time management, and decision making.

You know how your brain sometimes feels like it's full of hundreds of thoughts all at the same time? In my experience, this can lead to procrastination and distraction since it's hard to focus on just one thing for very long. However, I've found that my ability to manage tasks has been strengthened by better executive function.

Executive Functioning: What is It and How Can It Help Me?

Executive functioning, or EF, is simply a set of skills that allows us to operate efficiently. Harvard researchers describe EF as an "air traffic control system" that attempts to smoothly manage the multiple, overlapping intellectual and emotional tasks we deal with every day. We like to think of Executive functioning as the CEO of our brains, who uses advanced skills to successfully run the business of our everyday lives.

These make up our executive function skill set. For everyone, this skill set strengthens over time through years of practice. The process begins when we're babies and continues well into young adulthood. Research shows that the part of the brain in charge of EF—the prefrontal cortex, which is located directly behind your forehead—keeps developing all the way until our mid-20s.

It's important to realize that executive functioning skills are not related to intelligence. In fact, countless smart, successful adults struggle with EF and have created systems that work well for them. The more you practice EF skills and build strategies that work for you, the stronger they become. Learning and developing these techniques improves your EF and increases your confidence in navigating life's complexities.

In general, executive functioning means you are actively and skillfully using your mental abilities to manage life. Executive functioning includes:

- Problem solving
- Self-monitoring
- Planning/prioritizing
- Mental flexibility
- Working memory
- Gathering relevant information
- Filtering out distractions
- Assessing situations to determine the best course of action
- Remembering important details
- Organizing
- Controlling impulses
- Juggling our busy lives without dropping too many balls
- Helping manage and regulate our emotions

In your job, can you foresee a time where your employer would be glad that you have better executive function skills?

The better your executive functioning skills are, the more likely you will be able to do the tasks needed for your job successfully without supervision.

One of the main things that executive functioning helps with is shifting focus. So, if you have so many things going on at once, you need to be able to change focus from one thing to another as needed. I noticed this in myself during my first year of college when I had a lot of activities in my life. During the year, I developed bad habits about shifting my focus that lasted for years afterward.

In a nutshell, executive function skills help you stay on-task and avoid procrastination because they help you shift focus successfully from one thing to another when tasks are too daunting for you.

So, if you have so many things going on at once, you need to be able to change focus from one thing to another as needed. I noticed this in myself during my first year of college when I had a lot of activities in my life. During the year, I developed bad habits about shifting my focus that lasted for years afterward .

Is Executive Dysfunction an ADHD Symptom?

Executive dysfunction is a common symptom of Attention Deficit Hyperactivity Disorder (ADHD), but can it also be caused by other things? Executive dysfunction, or dyslexia-like syndrome, is a symptom of ADHD characterized by working memory difficulties with successful task completion. The most commonly reported symptoms are difficulty multi-tasking, difficulty planning, and difficulty staying on track. What causes this phenomenon in people with ADHD?

It's no secret that living with ADHD can be difficult: difficulty remembering important tasks, difficulty completing schoolwork, and general forgetfulness. While these symptoms are more commonly associated with ADHD in children, they are not restricted only to children; they can also affect adults who were diagnosed with ADHD when they were older.

The complex combination of symptoms that make up the disorder is referred to as executive dysfunction. As this term implies, it refers not just to problems focusing or unduly procrastinating but also difficulties sustaining focus on the task at hand and poor decision-making skills when it comes to areas like finances and relationships.

What causes it?

The extent to which someone is affected by executive dysfunction varies from person to person. Some people have only mild symptoms or very few problems, while others may exhibit a great deal of difficulty. In some cases, the cause of executive dysfunction is unknown and genetics may play a role. For example, ADHD is often genetic and there is evidence that part of the reason why one in five people with ADHD also has bipolar disorder (which has its own set of difficulties) is because they inherited the same genes.

It is also possible that executive dysfunction may be triggered by injury to the brain as a result of something like a car accident, resulting in a traumatic brain injury (TBI). It is estimated that about 10-15% of Americans have sustained some sort of TBI and many have no idea because they never received an official diagnosis.

What are the signs and symptoms of executive dysfunction?

The symptoms associated with executive dysfunction include:

Being forgetful, distracted, or having trouble following through on tasks. (This may be caused by things like a poor attention span or lack of motivation.)

Lack of focus and being easily distracted. (This may be caused by issues with organization.)

Difficulty organizing tasks, keeping track of information, and staying on task. This makes it difficult to complete projects in a timely manner and/or procrastinate. (These symptoms can be caused by issues such as poor planning skills, an inability to prioritize or organize things well or having little to no patience. These symptoms can sometimes be caused by issues such as zero-tolerance policies at school or in the workplace, which make it difficult to cope with situations that require some lenience.)

Having trouble completing a task satisfactorily or doing tasks without making mistakes. (This may be caused by a lack of ability in areas such as math, spelling, or handwriting.)

Difficulty focusing on details (e.g., having trouble following directions). (This is often due to a lack of focus and/or being easily distracted.)

Having difficulty holding onto new information (this may cause someone to struggle academically).

Being slow at processing information and taking longer than usual to complete tasks. This can be caused by issues such as an inability to concentrate or not following directions.

Having trouble organizing information and keeping things in order or having too much going on at once (e.g., trying to complete too many tasks at one time). (This may be due to a lack of ability in areas such as short-term memory.)

Being easily frustrated, unable to cope with stress, and/or having difficulty starting or finishing things (this is often a result of issues such as organization difficulties and planning skills).

Behaving impulsively, making bad decisions about money,

abusing substances, having problems at work or school, and/or making poor choices about friends. This may be due to issues with impulse control.

Being easily influenced by others or being ruled by their emotions. This can be a result of issues with organization, planning and prioritizing skills, and/or impulse control.

What are the causes of executive dysfunction?

While everyone experiences executive dysfunction to a certain extent, the cause of executive dysfunction varies greatly from person to person. Some common causes include:

Brain injury (e.g., due to a car accident, TBI [traumatic brain injury]) or an illness (e.g., arthritis) that results in an inability to concentrate or think clearly. This can cause a disturbance in the functioning of regions of the brain that process the use of short-term memory and other parts of the brain (e.g., parts of the frontal lobe).

Mental illness (e.g., bipolar disorder, schizophrenia) that results in flashbacks, hallucinations, or delusions. This can affect a person's ability to think clearly and/or logically.

Tourette syndrome (TS), attention deficit hyperactivity disorder with aggressive features, or conduct disorder. These conditions are associated with experiencing strange symptoms such as vocal tics, worsening inattention and hyperactivity.

Stroke. A stroke, which is the interruption of blood flow to a part of the body, can damage brain tissue and affect the parts of the brain that are responsible for memory, processing information and making decisions.

How is executive dysfunction diagnosed?

Most people who experience executive dysfunction don't

receive an official diagnosis; more likely than not there will be no record in their medical history that they were ever diagnosed with anything. This is because many people with problems like ADHD will only receive a diagnosis as children and/or teens.

When it comes to executive dysfunction, most people with the symptoms listed above (and sometimes even people who don't meet all the criteria) will be diagnosed with ADD and/or ADHD. In some cases, those with executive dysfunction may be misdiagnosed as having depression or another mental illness. Regardless of this diagnosis, the diagnosis that a person receives for executive dysfunction is very different from their diagnosis for any other condition their may have. Many medications are used to treat ADHD and ADD but not recommended for use on people with executive dysfunction as they can cause problems such as side effects, dependency, or just don't work well anyway. A person with executive dysfunction needs to work with a psychiatrist, neuropsychologist, or someone else who specializes in treating executive dysfunction if they are interested in the possibility of trying medications for executive dysfunction.

Are there any treatment options?

The best treatment option for those who have experienced executive dysfunction is not medication but rather working with someone who can teach them how to better deal with stress and remain organized. For example, some people may benefit from learning how to better manage their bills or planning for trips or big purchases. Work on improving organizational skills, planning skills, and learning how to prioritize tasks and stay on task will help anyone improve their executive functioning. In addition to working on organizational skills, it is also very important for those who are interested in doing something about their identification as having executive dysfunction to learn about the causes of executive dysfunction and the backgrounds of people who have experienced executive dysfunction.

Executive Function and ADHD Brain

Executive function is a general term for the brain's ability to prioritize, plan, inhibit impulse, and remember. It is also commonly referred to as "self-regulation." In other words, executive function helps you learn how to use your brain properly and stay focused on what you're doing.

Some of the most common cognitive behavioral tools for improving executive function are meditation, deep breathing exercises, and mindfulness. However, these are only effective if they are combined with an appropriate physical activity — like finding a way to physically move your body during meditation.

One of the most interesting things about executive function is the role it plays in ADHD. The symptoms of ADHD can take a toll on every area of a person's life, especially their executive function. For example, they will have difficulty completing tasks (such as paying bills or following directions), doing homework, making plans, and organizing their time.

In addition, people with ADHD may find it difficult to finish tasks even when they've started them weeks in advance. This inability to finish tasks is known as procrastination and is a very common symptom among people with ADHD. Some even go as far as making plans and then completely forgetting about them.

However, people with ADHD tend to have a relatively good working memory and multitasking ability. This makes them excellent candidates for jobs in computer programming, engineering, and gaming. In games such as Starcraft II or World of Warcraft, the best players have "good memories" that enable them to play several weeks of games without having to stop playing.

So why do people with ADHD tend to have an above average working memory? To answer this question we must first turn our attention towards the brain malfunctions that can cause low executive function in people with ADHD. As we've discussed above, ADHD is a very common neurodevelopmental disorder. Approximately 9 percent of children in the United States are diagnosed with ADHD.

While the majority of children diagnosed with ADHD will grow out of it, some have problems growing out of it as adults. In most cases of adult ADHD, the brain malfunctions that were present during childhood are still present. However, most people with adult ADHD do not realize they have an illness and continue to live their lives symptom free.

In other cases, sometimes a person may not develop any symptoms until they reach adulthood. These cases may make them appear younger than their actual ages or smaller than average.

The most common symptom of ADHD is a lack of impulse control, or being over-reactive to stimuli. This trait can cause ADHD sufferers to have an inability to maintain their attention span, causing a lot of fidgeting and moving about during the day. This can make them look like hyperactive children and may sometimes lead them to be misdiagnosed with ADHD in adulthood.

ADHD is believed to be caused by a combination of hereditary factors, environmental factors (like certain foods), and brain malfunctions. However, until about two years ago, our understanding of how brain malfunctions contribute to the symptoms of ADHD was very limited.

Recently, however, a team of researchers from the University of Pittsburgh and the University of Oregon used functional magnetic resonance imaging (fMRI) to examine the brain malfunctions that may cause poor executive function in people with ADHD.

While conducting this study they found that people with

ADHD showed reduced activity in their prefrontal cortexes. These are located behind the forehead and are commonly known as "executive" or "lobes." In other words, they found that people with ADHD have reduced activity in their "executive network."

The implications of this study are huge. For example, it helps explain why people with ADHD have trouble maintaining their focus and have a low attention span. In addition, the findings of this study may help researchers develop more accurate ways to diagnose ADHD in adulthood.

Currently, most doctors use the same diagnostic criteria to diagnose adults with ADHD as they do children. This can sometimes lead to misdiagnoses in adults because children and adults may manifest different symptoms for the disease.

For example, a child's symptoms may include hyperactivity and trouble staying focused on tasks. However, an adult with ADHD may often times not exhibit any of these symptoms but instead show greater impairments when it comes to working memory and attention span.

The researchers behind the study hope that their findings will help doctors have a better understanding of brain malfunctions in ADHD. By studying the differences between children and adults with ADHD, doctors may be able to develop more accurate diagnostic tools for working with patients of all ages.

The findings of this study also open up new lines of treatment for adult ADHD sufferers. Treatment options will be greatly increased if diagnosis is improved and more effective medications are developed to target specific symptoms of adult ADHD.

However, the biggest implication of this study is that doctors will have an improved understanding of how ADHD may manifest in adulthood. This will lead to better treatment options and diagnoses for adult ADHD sufferers.

The most common type of medication used to treat children with ADHD is a stimulant medication such as Ritalin or Adderall. These medications can help ADHD symptoms by boosting the person's attention and working memory, but they do not target the problem at its source.

In most cases, lack of executive function is not caused by a lack of attention and working memory; rather it is due to a specific brain malfunction know as developmental dyslexia which has been recognized since William's time.

Unfortunately, most doctors do not understand the principles of dyslexia and how it can cause poor executive function in people with ADHD. This is why many adults with ADHD are unaware of the fact that they may have an underlying brain malfunction and therefore, do not receive any treatment for it.

Chapter 4: What Challenges are Faced by Adults with ADHD?

Individuals with ADHD may face unique challenges and disadvantages because of their disorder. They may be more susceptible to and less likely to seek treatment for substance abuse and mental health disorders, such as anxiety and depression. They also often experience challenges with executive functioning skills, such as organization and time management, which can negatively affect their careers. On the brighter side, many people with ADHD have a strong need for novelty as well as a good memory for information that has been deemed important or interesting by them or someone else.

This article lists the most common challenges faced by adults with ADHD. The challenges are listed in alphabetical order, based on their starting theme.

Lack of sleep or sleep deprivation is linked to a variety of physical and mental problems, including hormonal changes and poor immune system functioning which can increase the risk of cardiovascular disease and diabetes. It has been reported that individuals with ADHD tend to have irregular sleeping patterns, with either insomnia or hypersomnia. The average adult spends about seven hours a night sleeping; however, children with ADHD may spend anywhere from four to ten hours getting adequate rest. When asked why they couldn't sleep, more than two thirds of patients with ADHD said it was because their minds were racing too much to fall asleep.

The likelihood of having a psychiatric comorbidity is considerably higher for those with ADHD, but this does not mean that all patients with ADHD have another disorder. Anxiety disorders are the most common comorbidities in children and adults with ADHD, occurring in roughly two thirds of individuals. Depression occurs in about half of those with adult ADHD; the risk of suicide attempt is at least double the general population. Substance abuse disorders are also more frequent in individuals with ADHD; however, these rates may be inflated due to methodological problems associated with their diagnosis.

Individuals with ADHD also have a higher risk of receiving a diagnosis of bipolar disorder than those in the general population. The rate of attention deficit hyperactivity disorder is estimated to be around 2.5% in children and 4% in adults, while the rate of bipolar disorder is estimated to be around 1.5%. As noted by one study, "It has been speculated that psychostimulants likely mediate the etiology of ADHD as well as its comorbidity with subthreshold psychotic symptoms, whereas dopamine antagonists may serve as medications for bipolar disorders."

Recently, there has been interest in using transcranial magnetic stimulation (TMS) for treating ADHD. A recent Cochrane review shows that TMS has some effectiveness in treating adult ADHD. The review showed that the effect was "very small" and that other non-medication treatments should be considered before using TMS.

While there are no specific stimulant medications available to treat ADHD without a prescription, there are several over-the-counter (OTC) options available for adults with ADHD or those who want to self-medicate. These include Adderall XR and Concerta. Adderall, a potent amphetamine, is used by approximately 50% of children with ADHD; however, for adults it is not considered as effective as the long-acting version, Adderall long acting.

The long-term use of amphetamines may lead to physical dependence, psychological dependence, and abuse. Both amphetamine and methylphenidate are associated with increase in metabolism, increased blood pressure and heart rate, insomnia, decreased appetite, dry mouth and sweating. In the short term, both can result in a "high," with the user feeling more alert; in prolonged use however it may cause irritability or even psychosis. Newer formulations of ADHD medications are less likely to be abusable than earlier versions.

Compared to placebo or the active control (amphetamine), atomoxetine was superior on most primary and secondary measures at all time points during the acute treatment phase (weeks 1 through 6). It was generally well tolerated, with the most common adverse events being decreased appetite, insomnia, nausea, and vomiting.

While there is no cure for ADHD, symptoms can be managed through medication and behavioral therapy. Approximately 70% of children respond to stimulants; however these medications only provide about a small to moderate effect size over placebo for all symptoms of ADHD. The use of stimulants among adults with ADHD is more controversial; since these drugs can cause addiction and cardiovascular damage in adults. Stimulant treatment has not been found to have a significant effect on the underlying neurobiology of ADHD.

Behavioral therapy can improve and change negative patterns, thoughts, and actions related to failure and success. Among the strategies used are: maintaining a consistent routine, monitoring progress, building confidence, encouraging self-sufficiency, setting goals and providing immediate feedback. Behavioral therapy can also help an adult with ADHD improve their social skills by teaching them how to handle situations such as being criticized in a meeting or giving a presentation. For some adults this therapy is so effective that they are able to manage most or all of their symptoms without medication.

Simple daily activities such as picking up kids from game

practices or finishing a job project on time may become very difficult for people with attention deficit hyperactivity disorder (ADHD). Chronic hyperactivity, difficulty concentrating, not having a track of time, procrastination and interrupting others are some of the identifications of this disorder linked to derailment in everyday life. The only good news is that, with very little forethought and a few easy changes, you may begin to overcome the difficulties presented by this disorder right now.

1. Being Late for Appointments Is a Challenge

Regular punctuality is a challenge for people with attention deficit disorder, whether it is about picking up children after a playdate, getting to some doctor's appointment, or even keeping on time at work. You may have trouble with managing time—5 minutes might seem like ten, and vice versa—or people might find themselves wasting time performing mundane activities like searching through their wardrobe for clothing.

2. Objects Are Often Being Misplaced Which Is a Challenge

You cannot find your keys and mobile phone and any other accessory when you need them? Adults with this disorder are prone to misplacing or completely losing such things, a frequent symptom.

3. Noise Is a Constant Source of Distraction

The presence of background noise which people who do not have ADHD may not even notice—such as that of radio or television broadcasts at home, or anywhere including at work, or even at some restaurant—may be very distracting for those who have ADHD since they are unable to shut it out.

4. Getting Adequate Sleep Is a Difficult Task

According to the National Sleep Foundation, many people with attention deficit disorder have difficulty sleeping and it is difficult for them to react to internal signals that indicate that it is time to calm down and prepare themselves for bed. Even closer tonight, you may find yourself gaining momentum. Adults having ADHD are more likely to be night owls, according to Dr. Wetzel.

5. Keeping Up with Paperwork Is a Challenge

Is your work desk covered by a mountain of paperwork, with vital documents getting lost among the jumbled piles? Managing paperwork seems tedious, but deciding whether to save it or discard it requires a degree of attention that any adult with ADHD may be unable to muster.

6. Keeping Yourself Safe on the Road Is a Challenge

According to research, people with attention deficit hyperactivity disorder (ADHD) had way greater risks of traffic accidents and infractions than any other typical adult.

7. Maintaining Conversations Is a Difficult Task

You tend to complete other people's sentences as if you already know exactly what the other person is going to say next, don't you? For people with ADHD who are always impatient, having meaningful discussions may be challenging.

8. Keeping Track of Tasks While on the Job Is a Challenge

Just because the paper on which meeting with one of your employers was written has been misplaced, you are unable to recall whether the meeting began at 9 a.m. or 10 a.m. If you get home from work, you have no idea if it is your time to go for soccer practice today or do you have to go tomorrow. Does this sound familiar?

9. Prioritizing Your Day Is a Difficult Task

Knowing what you need to do first may be difficult when your planner is overflowing, and you're dealing with adult attention deficit disorder. This can make a very stressful start to the day.

10. Completing Tasks Is a Difficult Task

Having adult ADHD makes it difficult to complete tasks, especially when you are just concentrating on a small number of assignments at once. "People were having ADHD begin activities and other projects with a great deal of energy and enthusiasm, but as soon as the project progresses, that energy and enthusiasm may wane," Wetzel says.

Gender and ADHD

The intersection of ADHD and gender is a very complicated one. Men are more likely to be diagnosed with ADHD than women, but that's primarily because men are more likely to have hyperactive symptoms that lead them to be noticed by parents, teachers, and other adults who might not otherwise diagnose the disorder. But in young girls, inattentive symptoms tend to dominate their presentation of the disorder. Girls also tend to come into treatment much later because they show less disruptive behavior.

We will cover many factors relevant for understanding how ADHD presents differently in males versus females, both during the course of the condition as well as across diagnosis rates at different ages. A number of studies show that attention and hyperactive/impulsive symptoms are gender-matched, while girls present with a greater degree of inattentive symptoms. In addition, there are differences in the way ADHD seems to express itself in males versus females (as well as cultural factors), so we will also examine some of these reports.

Gender Differences in Testosterone and ADHD Symptoms

A interesting study was conducted recently by researchers at the University of Amsterdam which examined the influence of testosterone on ADHD symptoms. The study recruited 36 boys and 36 girls who had been diagnosed with hyperactivity disorder (ADHD) or other disruptive behavior disorders. These boys and girls were given a testosterone gel containing 0 mg of testosterone, 10 mg of testosterone, or a placebo. The children were given this therapy over the course of two weeks.

The researchers conducted several measures of ADHD symptoms including the Home Situations Questionnaire (HSQ), which is used to assess hyperactive and impulsive behavior in children aged 4-6 years old, and the Conners' Parent Rating Scale which is used to measure ADHD symptoms in children aged 6-12 years old. The ADHD Rating Scale from the Diagnostic and Statistical Manual IV was also used to gauge overall severity of symptoms.

The results showed that girls had higher levels of inattentive symptoms than boys and that testosterone did not have a significant impact on their symptoms. In contrast, ADHD symptoms were generally lower in the group who received 3 mg of the testosterone gel (versus those who received 0 mg or 10 mg) and hyperactive/impulsive symptoms were reduced even more due to this amount of the hormone. In addition, boys had higher levels of hyperactive/impulsive symptoms than girls, but as with past studies, this observation was primarily due to the fact that there were simply more males in the study than females.

Here we can see evidence for gender differences in ADHD expression as well as for testosterone's influence on ADHD symptom severity. In general, girls present with more inattentive symptoms and boys with more hyperactive/impulsive ones. This could be because whitespace is more important to girls than boys (at least until they're adolescents!) or that over the course of evolution females have developed a more sensitive system for detecting disruption in social interactions. Nevertheless, testosterone seems to increase hyperactive/impulsive symptoms in both genders and this could be a possible cause for its influence on symptom severity.

There are also cultural factors at play here as well: ADHD tends to be diagnosed less frequently in countries where women are given greater autonomy or where there's generally a lower ratio of males to females. (It's also interesting to note that hyperactivity was more frequently diagnosed in countries where there were more females in the sample at the beginning of the study.)

Gender Differences in Mood and Symptoms

Most studies show a higher prevalence of inattentive symptoms and depressive symptoms among males with ADHD than females. There could be a reason for that, namely that it's hard to keep things organized when your mind is going 1000 mph. It's also possible that part of the reason women seem less interested in taking ADHD medications is because they see it as a "masculine disorder", or as a symptom of weakness.

In one study , researchers at the Université de Montréal observed that 60% of girls and 63.3% of boys with ADHD had mood disorders, but the researchers also concluded that this was because most people presenting with ADHD were being treated with antidepressants. This can be "masking" the higher prevalence of mood disorders among females with ADHD.

In addition, some studies have shown how boys present more frequently than girls in childhood and then switch to having more girls presenting in adolescence although there's no real consensus on this issue.

Pregnancy

Since there's some research suggesting that women with ADHD have a hard time getting pregnant, it's easier to focus on how this manifests itself during pregnancy. (Other studies show that women do not have an increased risk of ADHD during pregnancy.)

In a study from Italy, researchers followed 21 women with ADHD through pregnancy and found that the majority of them experienced symptoms of depression in their third trimester and the average symptom severity was twice as high in women with ADHD versus controls. In addition, 45% of the women reported hyperactive symptoms when they were pregnant compared to 22% who had never been pregnant before.

In another study , researchers examined the medical record of 34 women with ADHD and found that the most common comorbid conditions were anxiety disorders (20.6%), mood disorders (13.8%) and substance abuse/dependence (12.8%).

Some researchers have argued that inattentive symptoms are frequently associated with postpartum depression, but numerous studies show this to be true for all types of depression, not just cases related to childbirth. Nevertheless, there is research to suggest that women who receive treatment for postpartum depression are more likely to experience inattentive symptoms than their untreated counterparts.

There is no male or female type of ADHD, although women tend to exhibit traits of one of the subgroups of ADHD more than the others, the inattentive type. The more science learns about ADHD and its differences in men and women, the lesser the gap in its diagnosis. The inattentive form of ADHD is most common in girls, and since it has more internalized symptoms, it often goes unnoticed. Science and research have a lot of information on ADHD and its symptoms; however, this information is more based on boys than girls. Because there is ample information about the topic, it often gives us the notion of knowing enough about it; however, it is not the case at all in women with ADHD. Unlike men, women tend to also get comorbid disorders that show up at the same time as ADHD. This will often divert clinicians from diagnosing ADHD itself. Comorbid disorders could be personality disorders, eating disorders and substance use.

During puberty, girls will have an exacerbation of symptoms associated with ADHD because of the drop in hormone levels. They would have lower estrogen levels that will, in turn, trigger more irritability, mood disruption, sleep disturbances and concentration issues. Young women with ADHD have lower levels of self-efficacy and poorly cope with general life situations. Whilst physical aggression and other externalized behaviors tend to be higher in men and boys, depression and anxiety are higher in girls. Men will show external frustration while women will direct their pain and anger inwards. Women with undiagnosed ADHD are at a higher risk of experiencing problems in school, social setups and relationships than neurotypical girls. Men with ADHD would typically be more hypersensitive, are unable to concentrate and tend to change jobs more frequently. Women with ADHD will note psychological distress, low self-esteem and feelings of incapacity. Women with ADHD will likely face time-management challenges, disorganization, overwhelm, struggle with money management alongside a history of anxiety and depression.

Women with ADHD tend to suffer from a separation anxiety disorder, also known as SAD, while men will be more likely to have an oppositional defiant disorder. SAD is a disorder characterized by anxiety where one experiences excessively concerning levels of separation from home or individuals with whom they hold a strong connection. This will have them feeling extremely sad and have difficulty focusing when away from the people they love or away from their comfortable environment. Oppositional defiant disorder, also known as ODD, is more characterized by repeated patterns of irritability, anger, arguing and maliciousness. People suffering from ODD easily and often lose their temper and are often resentful. They may refuse to comply with rules or obey authoritative bodies. The fact that women often experience SAD and men experience ODD is greatly influenced by gender roles and societal expectations.

While women with ADHD may experience some of the same symptoms experienced by their male counterparts, women still have to endeavor under the imposed burden and restrictions imposed on gender roles. They have to deal with fluctuating hormones, unlike men, resulting in a higher tendency to self-doubt and self-harm. Although at face value, women and men with ADHD may display similar symptoms, in the long term, women will face conclusively different fallouts. As a practical example, if a female with ADHD is disorganized and forgetful to the point where if she forgets to pick up her children from school, she may be perceived as lacking motherly instincts and disregarding her duties as a mother. A man will be more accepted in society to be disorganized and forgetful primarily because women are "assigned" to be homemakers. They are the ones expected to set appointments, take care of the house chores and the children. If a mother is fidgeting late to her child's first school play, it may be easily mistaken for her disordered life. Women may still try hard to hide these flaws and may be afraid to ask for help. They will often end up doubting themselves and back off when their integrity is questioned.

Women with ADHD rely heavily on their intelligence to compensate for their flaws, all the while struggling to maintain focus. This makes them question their abilities overall. Succeeding can require bigger portions of their energy and time. They often compare themselves to others who always seem to achieve more than them effortlessly. They are forced to self-monitor continuously and strive for perfection. They can spend most of their time preparing obsessively, and if they overlook minor details, they beat themselves up, making themselves feel unworthy of love and compassion.

The disastrous combination of internalized symptoms, hormonal changes and societal pressure creates a series of stressors exclusive to females with ADHD. Women with ADHD can perceive their negative experiences more agonizingly than men. They are more likely to struggle with low self-esteem than men and feel lucky if things turn out well for them instead of praising themselves for a job well done. If we take the experiences of men with ADHD as a standard, we will fail to understand women with ADHD and how to diagnose them altogether. It may be more helpful to equate women with ADHD to women who do not have the disorder because this analysis can be done based on one variable, the condition. If men and women with ADHD are compared, you are more likely to miss traits in women because, as already established, women's symptoms exhibit themselves differently than men's.

How to Diagnose ADHD in Women

If you are wondering how to diagnose ADHD in women, the first thing to do is figure out what symptoms may be present in your patient. For example, if giving a presentation at work is difficult for your patient, this would be a part of the diagnostic criteria. You could also use examples such as being easily distracted, having trouble with organization, or arguing about trivial things in relationships as further indicators that your patient may have ADHD.

When it comes to ADHD, there are many myths and misconceptions that are often held by the public. One of these is that women don't have ADHD, which is absolutely false. And yet this myth perpetuates itself in society because girls who do have ADHD face a unique problem: they're being undiagnosed and let down by the health care industry.

Women with ADHD tend to present differently from men, often presenting as more emotionally sensitive, and having a harder time regulating negative emotions. Often their behavior works best when they're in a stable environment and can exercise greater self-control. These tips will help you find out whether the person you're dealing with has ADHD, or another condition that could be causing their unusual symptoms

Did you know that one of the most important signs of ADHD is how someone reacts to stress? It's not unusual for people with ADHD to lash out or become physically aggressive when under pressure.

Women with ADHD tend to have the inattentive type of this disorder, as said before. There would be, of course, women who have the hyperactive-impulsive type, which will get these women diagnosed earlier in life as the symptoms they exhibit are more commonly associated with ADHD. Imagine giving a woman the responsibility to take care of her family and kids over and above the duties she has already been assigned, like pursuing a career. They already struggle with organizing and taking control over their life; any further duties would be too much. This places an even bigger burden on women with ADHD and they often come across as the ones that do not perform well enough.

Healthcare professionals can take various approaches to diagnose ADHD. There is no right or wrong test for this, and often, a psychiatrist or a therapist will diagnose you after a series of assessments. Guidelines ask specialists to also consider the severity of the condition. This varies depending on how it manifests itself over the course of a person's life. Clinicians may categorize ADHD intensity as mild, moderate, or severe. Mild can mean that few symptoms are present, and these symptoms minimally impair the sufferer in a social setting. Moderate ADHD means symptoms have a functional impairment and are usually more powerful than those presented in mild cases of ADHD. Severe ADHD can mean symptoms are present heavily and are highly interfere with one's life at work, in a relationship, at school, or at home. Individuals' symptoms can diminish, improve, or take on new forms as they mature. Adults that retain any but not all of the signs of childhood ADHD can be diagnosed with ADHD in partial remission.

Diagnosing adult women with ADHD varies from diagnosing young children, so is the diagnostic approach taken by clinicians. The specialist gathers more information from you about your present symptoms. At present, clinicians are guided to verify whether symptoms were present in childhood; if otherwise, a confirmed diagnosis of ADHD cannot be given. If this cannot be confirmed because someone may be unsure about signs and symptoms present years ago, the specialist might want to review your school records, speak to your previous teachers and consult your parents or guardians.

For a definitive diagnosis to be made, one must display the effects of their symptoms during their day-to-day activities, such as dangerous driving, underachieving at work or school, struggle to maintain friendships and relationships. Questionnaires and psychological tests are also performed by a specialist to help diagnose ADHD. At present, guidelines indicate one must have at least five or more symptoms to be diagnosed with ADHD and these symptoms must interfere with their day-to-day living. In adults, symptoms need to be traced back to childhood and your therapist or specialist will help you identify these issues from the past. In the clinic room, you will also identify how often these symptoms appear and in which settings they often exhibit.

A diagnosis in adult women is mostly made from the individual's history, but other methods may be used, such as continuous performance tests, checking for impulsivity or attention problems and brain scans. Social, medical and family history are all assessed during one-on-one consultations with your clinician. This will help determine the challenges you seem to face in your life and underlying medical conditions that may be mistaken for symptoms of ADHD. Completing an ADHD rating scale test will help determine whether an adult has ADHD and if they also have other issues like learning disabilities, auditory disorders, or mood disorders. These tests may take from a couple of hours to multiple days, depending on the clinician's approach and the extent of the condition. An intelligence test may also be performed to test one's IQ and help identify other learning disabilities. If a mood disorder is suspected, a broad-spectrum scale test may also be performed to help identify other emotional or psychiatric problems such as obsessive-compulsive disorder. Depending on the outcome of these tests, one might opt to perform other specific tests to test abilities like motor skills or memory recall. Computer tests for ADHD are also becoming a trend, primarily because sufferers enjoy taking them. These will screen them for impulsivity and attention problems. Continuous performance tests, known as CPT, challenge people to maintain attention throughout. Targets will appear on the screen and the users need to respond to these targets. The system records their ability to stay on task.

Diagnosing ADHD is purely based on a clinical evaluation as there are no laboratory-based tests that will help diagnose

ADHD, such as blood tests. Different physicians can have different approaches to diagnosing ADHD and this can depend on their resources and their preferred methods.

All in all, taking the first step in the right direction is what matters the most. Seeing your trusted practitioner is all it takes to get you started and eventually get you the help you need.

What Happens in Woman With ADHDLeft Undiagnosed

Missing a diagnosis for any condition can be devastating for one's physical and mental health, including ADHD. By now, we have very well established why and how women are mostly undiagnosed or misdiagnosed with ADHD more often than men. Women will get a diagnosis mostly when they enter adulthood and start taking up heavier responsibilities like running a family or working a career. This may result in frequent trips to the psychiatrist, only to be told they have depression or anxiety and be treated for these conditions; however, they would notice that the problem remains.

Women with undiagnosed ADHD tend to have different manifestations than men, such as eating disorders, anxiety, depression and low self-esteem, as extensively discussed. The inattentive type of undiagnosed ADHD in women can result in teen pregnancy, higher rates of dropouts in school and a higher risk of getting fired from their job. Undiagnosed women may be prone to more frequent career changes. If you have been misdiagnosed with ADHD or not diagnosed at all, you may tend to let your bills go unpaid and not run errands properly. A series of these events leave women feeling disappointed because they are not completing tasks as expected of them.

Women with undiagnosed ADHD may experience rejection-sensitive dysphoria, also known as RSD. This is an emotional sensitivity and pain usually triggering a notion of rejection and criticism caused by the most important people in one's life. This can also be caused by a sense of failing to meet expectations or being unable to fulfill standards either imposed on oneself or imposed by others. This does not mean that ADHD sufferers with RSD are too sensitive or unable to handle criticism but rather have an amplified emotional response compared to people without this condition. No one likes criticism or that feeling of rejection; however, people with ADHD and RSD have a more severe reaction to criticism and this may highly impair their lives. Because the emotional response of RSD is internalized, it will often be portrayed as a mood disorder, with occasional suicidal ideation. Think of someone who is feeling perfectly fine at a given moment and immensely sad in the next. This results in diagnosing individuals with cycling mood disorders rather than ADHD. It might take time for clinicians to make a correct and accurate diagnosis in these instances because RSD is very common in adults with ADHD. This emotional response can also be externalized, often seeming like instant rage towards the person responsible for causing such emotional pain.

Women, whose ADHD goes undiagnosed, may also experience emotional dysregulation. This may manifest itself in both sexes and in different ways. One way is getting easily irritated and having a minuscule emotional threshold. Anything can set them off, and they get upset with the smallest of things. Certain information may rub them the wrong way. Most women with ADHD may also be introverts, leaving them to feel trapped by the circumstances that they are in and bottle up their emotions. They would often feel they are invisible to others. Although they might commit to something they love or enjoy doing, that feeling at the back of their mind will still lure them into perceiving themselves as losers and good-for-nothing. Keep in mind, these young women would have been called names throughout their childhood because their symptoms and behaviors were misconceived.

Women with undiagnosed ADHD can often experience executive dysfunction. Executive function is a set of skills used to perform tasks such as paying attention, remembering information and multitasking. Neurotypical individuals use these skills to plan, organize, pay attention and manage their time effectively. These skills start developing from the ripe age of two and continue to fully evolve till the age of thirty. These skills are important in daily life and at the workplace. Executive dysfunction will make it harder for the individual to follow through on plans, remember things, abide by complex or detailed instructions and execute a project or a task they have been assigned. Women with ADHD who also have executive dysfunction may misplace things, struggle with their time management, be unable or struggle to organize schedules and stick to them, struggle with dealing with setbacks and frustration and be unable to self-monitor emotions or behavior. This weakness in your brain's self-management system means that your day-to-day tasks will be affected.

This will mean that errands or things around the house may not get done as often as they should or sometimes not at all. It can sometimes be the case that important things one needs to prioritize will often get put aside for much less important things. The latter might be something the sufferer finds much more fun and engaging, consequently resulting in the release of dopamine in the brain. Dopamine is a chemical produced by the body and used by your nervous system. Dopamine plays a role in the way we feel, and it affects moods and feelings of motivation and rewards. Because it helps us feel pleasure, it helps us find things that are interesting to us. Dopamine plays an even bigger role in mental health. Lack of dopamine levels will cause a lack of motivation and desire. ADHD itself may be exacerbated by a shortage of dopamine levels.

In a nutshell, this can be described as feelings and emotions that never switch off, making you constantly distracted and unable to focus. This might contribute to not getting much done at the end of it all. Neurodiverse people will thrive in the right environment and when surrounded by the right support system. Taking entrepreneurs as an example, people with ADHD tend to be self-employed or entrepreneurs. Many adults with ADHD opt to be self-employed because they tend to be more creative and have an entrepreneurial spirit. Others may struggle with getting or holding a job. Being their own boss will give them a more flexible schedule and may allow them to delegate tasks they are not so good at completing themselves. Although self-employment or entrepreneurship will present its set of challenges, it may provide the right flexibility for women with ADHD.

Most Effective Methods That Work for Coping with ADHD

There is no denying that ADHD is one of the most difficult things to live with in our society. It's a condition that affects 5-10% of school-aged children and often times can be quite difficult to control. In order to cope with ADHD, it's important that we examine the different ways in which people handle this condition and address them as appropriate. Read on for my list of effective methods for coping with this disorder, along with a review of each one. I've included a few of the most effective techniques that I've found to be helpful, provide my own personal take on them.

Some methods to help you cope with ADHD:

Get Diagnosed

If you suspect having ADHD, make getting a diagnosis a priority. You are more likely to forgive yourself for the shortcomings you had in the past and have more control over your current life. There is a condition for what you are going through, and getting diagnosed can give you a sense of relief. It is not a death sentence to have ADHD; it is a result of the way the brain is wired and understanding how it works can help you lead a better life.

Make Self-Care a Habitude!

If you have ADHD, you are probably hyper-focused to a point where you forgot to eat, sleep, or use the restroom. Try checking in on yourself occasionally. It is accepted to work on the task for a long time because it needs to be finished, but if you know this can happen, try keeping snacks on your desk for when you get hungry. Make frequent visits to the grocery shop and make sure you opt for healthy snacks and not junk food. Try getting up in the morning and getting ready for a day's work by having a shower and making yourself breakfast, even if you are working from home. Start by decluttering your space and consider making your bed every morning even though you are not expecting anyone to come over. If you manage your health, then managing everything else just follows.

Get a Healthy Amount of Sleep!

If you are restless, you are more likely to have exacerbated ADHD symptoms. This can affect your attention span, memory and problem-solving skills. Issues with sleep issues are a common problem you might face and the cure can be as simple as a change of habit. If you are getting less sleep than you need, you are likely to be more irritable. Adding physical activity can help you get a restful night.

Identify Conditions Arising from ADHD

ADHD rarely exists on its own. If you have ADHD, you are very likely to have one or more other conditions. This should not be an alarming discovery, but rather, the goal is to raise awareness. If you are a woman with undiagnosed or misdiagnosed ADHD, you probably have already been diagnosed with these coexisting conditions before being diagnosed with ADHD itself. Identify what coexisting conditions you have and start treating each one directly. Sometimes symptoms of coexisting conditions can be disguised by symptoms of ADHD or the other way round. Other conditions coexisting with ADHD can be anxiety disorders, bipolar disorder, depression, personality disorders and substance use disorders. It is crucial to share all symptoms with your physician when discussing your ADHD symptoms as well. This can help your physician get a full diagnosis and give you the treatment you need.

Drive Carefully

Women with ADHD tend to feel very distracted and inattentive when driving. You can increase safety on the roads by opting for a manual transmission instead of an automatic one. This can help you become more engaged while driving, and you are less likely to switch your attention to something else other than driving. Try switching off your phone before you start driving and avoid using a headset. If music distracts you, remove your stereo system. Do not do recreational drugs and use alcohol before driving, as these can reduce your focus even more.

Learn the Art of Time Management!

If you are a woman with ADHD, you probably struggle with time management. You often miss deadlines and underestimate the power of time. You may struggle to anticipate how much time a task can take you to complete. If you also hyper-focus, you may devote your time and energy to one task leaving others undone. It can leave you feeling stressed and overwhelmed. Create a schedule and get organized. Try writing down the things you want to get done the night before and prioritize your list. Do consider your strengths and not only your weaknesses.

This will boost your self-esteem and confidence. If you start working on a task or plan to, allow some extra time than you anticipate it will take. Make use of timers or alarms; this way, you know for how long you need to work on a particular task whether you like doing it or not.

Physical Activity

If you have the hyperactive type of ADHD, you may highly benefit from this. Either way, exercise can help you be focused and calm. Physical activity is not only great for your health but also for your mind. This can help you channel your energy in the right way and can help you rest better at night.

Make Use of Pillboxes

If you are a woman with ADHD one medication, you may struggle to remember whether you have taken your medication or remembering to take it at all. Using a pillbox can help you stay alert for when your medication is running low because you would prepare a week's supply in advance. This can help you manage your filling of prescriptions better and avoid leaving you without treatment for some time. This can save you from carrying multiple boxes with you wherever you go. A pillbox can also keep you more organized, and if you forgot whether you have taken it or not, all you need to do is look back in your pillbox. There are pillboxes with timers within them if you feel like you have enough reminders on your phone.

Learn to Say No!

Women with ADHD tend to be people-pleasers and often feel anxious when saying no. Do not take more than you can handle as this can only leave you overwhelmed, stressed and anxious. If you want to help, try taking on tasks you know you enjoy and can complete. If you are asked to participate or commit, do not say yes straight away but postpone it and say you will think about it. If you commit as soon as you are asked, you are likely to say yes involuntarily, whereas if you give it some thought, you can make a more informed decision and only take on tasks you really want to.

Keep a Clock in Your Shower

You may not admit it, but you spend more time in your bathroom than you should. You can get carried away wondering about your next invention, or things you should have said. Keep a clock in your bathroom to help you stay on top of time and avoid getting carried away by unnecessary thoughts.

Look For Help!

If you feel you are struggling at any given task, do not be afraid to ask for help, email your superior for further instructions via email about that project, and if you are struggling in life in general, do not be afraid to seek help from a therapist if you feel like you need a little extra help together with your medication.

Some things are easier said than done! Knowing where to begin and what methods you need to apply to get better is what you need towards a better-navigated life with ADHD.

Part 2- 15 Strategies for Thriving with Distraction

Although many people with attention deficit hyperactivity disorder or ADHD struggle to stay on task, there are some strategies for thriving despite distractions. Below are list of thoughts and insights on distractions and ADHD.

-Distractions can manifest in many different ways for those dealing with this condition, but one way to tackle the problem is to remember that everyone has a three-minute "default timer." This means that if you just spend the allotted time working (no matter what) and then take a break, no one will be the wiser.

-It's also important not to get discouraged by why you need to set aside your distractions. You might want to read a magazine but you'll feel more productive if you work on your computer. You also don't feel like doing the tough math problem that's due tomorrow so you decide to watch a movie. These are very normal distractions that everyone encounters in their lives, but with ADHD it's just easier to get left behind.

-Distractions can come at anyone at any time which is why it's so detrimental for people who have ADHD to be left with lingering things that need to get done. It's impossible for anyone to avoid being distracted and if you struggle with ADHD this is probably more true for you.

-It's important to remember that we all have distractions in our lives from things like relationships, work, and bills. But if your life is consumed by these things then you will undoubtedly end up living in a constant state of distraction and overwhelm. Distractions are easy to ignore when we're well proportioned with everything else in our lives, but when we ignore the responsibilities of life we create an avalanche of chaos. A good life is lived in balance, so never let yourself be consumed by unnecessary distractions.

-It's also important to point out that distractions can actually be a good thing. We wouldn't want to exist in a world without distractions because this would be a very boring place to live. But if ADHD has affected you, it means that you struggle with the consequences of these distractions. This is something that requires an extra amount of resolve and discipline because it's not easy for everyone to recognize their own limits.

Starting With Yourself

• The first step towards tackling the distraction problem is to take action yourself. You can't expect other people to help you improve your life if it's not something you're willing to do yourself.

• If you don't like the distractions associated with ADHD then it's your job to change them. You can accomplish this goal by learning how to recognize and focus on things that really matter. This may take some time because there are so many distractions in our world that it's easy for us to lose sight of what's important.

• It can be helpful to write down your goals and the reasons why you want to achieve them. We often have an idea of what we want to accomplish but it's important to get explicit with the reasons why you want to achieve these goals.

• For example, if your problem is that you procrastinate on each and every assignment then you need to create a specific goal that directly addresses this problem: "I will not procrastinate on my assignments" or "I will complete my assigned tasks on time." If this is your goal then you can use discipline to keep yourself from doing other things that distract you.

- If you are a person who tends to get overwhelmed by work or school then it's important for you to understand what type of goals are important for those around you. For example, if you have a partner or roommate who needs to rely on you for getting things done then it's important for you to develop goals that are helpful in this situation.

- It can also be helpful to remember that you can't expect yourself to change overnight. Think of your ADHD as an addiction problem, but instead of using drugs or alcohol your main focus is on the tasks at hand.

- Some people may think that these goals are too simple, but the truth is that they are far more difficult to accomplish than we give ourselves credit for. Our minds like short term gratification and this goes against everything we want and need in our lives. Taking on a new goal can be a huge deal and you might feel discouraged at times, but it's important to stick with it.

- Just as every addiction causes us to struggle with our own personal demons we have to work through the process of overcoming our ADHD problems as well. If you have ADHD then you will inevitably have difficulties in your life; but if you're proactive about tackling these problems then you will come out stronger than ever.

- The Power of Peer Pressure

- One way that everyone struggles with distractions is because we follow the crowd. We look at our friends and see how they always seem to get everything done on time and don't think twice about how they do it.

- We tend to look at these people as if they have it all together, but this is often not the case. Chances are these people are struggling just like the rest of us because ADHD isn't always obvious.

- Try paying attention to your peers and try to find out what makes them so productive. They might not know why they're getting things done but looking for common traits can help you see what works for them and what doesn't.

- One thing that's crucial to realize is that we're all different from one another so we can't just copy other people's habits in order to meet our own goals. Just because someone else has a system set up doesn't mean that it will work for you.

- Another common mistake that people make is to forget how many different tasks they have to get done every day. If you take this approach then you'll end up with a ton of tasks in your life and it will be next to impossible for you to figure out what's important.

- Being productive is simply being able to accomplish the necessary tasks in a timely manner; so if you are truly capable of getting things done then there's no reason for you not to succeed. It helps if we realize that there's nothing more satisfying than finishing a project on time, but if we don't have this attitude then we're bound to live with distractions that stop us from achieving our goals.

- We all have a lot to do in our lives and ADHD isn't always the biggest problem to deal with. It's important for us to separate our struggles from our goals and make changes in order to reach these goals.

- If you have ADHD then you already know that you'll eventually be distracted from your important tasks.

Chapter 1: ADHD Women and Relationships

ADHD can be detrimental to relationships if both the sufferer and the partner are not appreciative and understanding of this condition. All the symptoms of ADHD like distraction, procrastination, forgetfulness, and fixation can cause havoc in the relationship, often leading to its termination. Symptoms of ADHD may cause frustration, anger, and hurt to both parties.

Because people with ADHD tend to suffer from executive dysfunction, they may often show up late for dates or meetings with their other half. This may come across as disrespectful to the other party and may be misinterpreted for lack of interest. People with ADHD tend to be forgetful and misplace things often, including personal belongings. If you text your partner, who suffers from ADHD, and do not hear back from them for a day or so, they probably forgot to respond to your text or call unintentionally, and they might have misplaced their phone. People with ADHD also suffer from sleep issues, so they might lack sleep or sleep too much. So, if you texted them to see where they wish to go for dinner and they are yet to reply, they could be napping. If you have ADHD and spend a big portion of your time looking for your wallet, keys, or phone, it is not because you are disorganized or a mess; it is probably because of your neurodiversity. The one suffering from ADHD may start avoiding their neurotypical partners as much as possible to avoid being criticized.

If your partner is the one suffering from ADHD, you may see them doing the same. Certain behaviors may not bother someone whilst dating, but in a long-term relationship, their actions will reflect their interest in the relationship and wherever it is headed. This can often lead to failed relationships and frequent break-ups. It is important to bear in mind that the behavior of an ADHD individual is not a reflection of how they feel about their other half or the relationship itself, but rather, symptoms of ADHD. Instead of blaming their partners for what seems to be the lack of skills, one should be more aware of their behavior and work on accepting the challenges someone with ADHD would experience.

Dating someone with ADHD can, in the beginning, be fun, instinctive and exciting. For a long-term relationship to work out, there needs to be mutual understanding and willingness. Remind your partner that they should not take your behavior personally because you probably do not intend to act the way you do and that you are harmless. Your neurotypical partner can feel devalued when you space out during a conversation, remind them that it is not intentional. Missing important details or committing to plans you forget or cannot honor later will make your partner feel ignored but making them aware of you and your condition should get them to understand your good intentions.

Inattention caused by ADHD in a relationship does not only mean losing stuff or spacing out during a conversation, but it can also mean getting bored. Boredom may be far more damaging to a relationship than misplacing your stuff.

People with ADHD look for things that are of personal interest and are challenging to them. They engage in new things, and ideally, these new challenging things have deadlines. All these factors contribute to firing up the dopamine levels in the brain. At the beginning of a relationship, the first three factors would all be present, making a relationship a new and challenging commitment, which all started because of the interest you had in each other. At the start of the relationship, people with ADHD can barely think about anything else except for this new commitment. All the attention and energy are lavished on their partner. As time goes by, the relationship may not be as stimulating as it was in the beginning, and people with a neurodiverse brain will shift their focus to ways to keep having fun with the hope to fire up their dopamine levels again. By this time, the non-ADHD partner would have gotten used to all the care and attention they were receiving, and as you can imagine, it will not feel good to them when you pull away. They may take it personally and might think you do not love them anymore. Before you start shifting to other things that will give you that dopamine kick, neurodiverse brains will do their best to preserve the relationship because they got hooked on the exclusive attention they received in the beginning. They can pretend everything is perfect in a relationship, even when it is obvious it is not. They want to preserve what is making them feel so good. If and once they realize that the relationship is not perfect, they may want to change the other person to protect it. In some instances, if boredom takes over, the ADHD partner may also turn to cheat and hope they do not hurt their partner and at the same time keep up the relationship whilst getting the high they need. With cheating comes lying; neurotypical individuals may lie to the other half with the same intent to keep up the relationship and avoid hurting the other.

If you are honest with each other and know where you stand, it will become less challenging because, although you will have to work out solutions to make it work for both of you, you will be working towards previously discussed goals. You will only get involved with people that are interested in you and vice versa. With constructive and open communication, you will constantly reinvent yourselves and the relationship. This creates a deeper connection between the parties, making it even more interesting. If you feel emotionally charged at any given moment, it is best if you take a break and walk away. It is vital to not bottle up emotions but rather deal with them as they come. It is essential to watch what you say, although this may be challenging if you are impulsive. Adding a little humor to the situation will lighten things up. Going in with the right mindset of listening to understand will completely reshape your perspective on issues.

This advice is for your partner: To help with communication in a relationship when one of the partners has ADHD, it will help if there are fixed times for discussions, so they are aware of the plans and are able to follow through a lot easier. It also helps to set up external reminders like whiteboards or sticky notes. Since people with ADHD get easily distracted, it is best if clutter is avoided around the house to help them stay focused. If you want to verify whether your partner with ADHD understood what you said, you can ask them to repeat the requests. Once this harmony is achieved, neurotypical brains can stop worrying about ending it, finding, or trying to save the relationship. This will enable people with ADHD to look for other things they can hyper-focus on other than the relationship and will be in it for their partner. Establishing the right support system in a relationship is essential to keep the relationship going. It is important to be compassionate and try to find the good in your partner.

It is understandable to mess up at times, and if both partners are fully invested and aware of each other, it will work out. One must work hard to prevent the relationship from becoming a co-dependent one, where only one partner is trying to make the relationship work. Make sure that duties and responsibilities are divided, and one party is not picking up too much slack for the other. It is understandable for tasks to be assigned to whoever does them best. People with ADHD may feel like they lack some skills and will feel more at ease to have certain tasks done by their other half.

If the load is divided equally and one does not feel more invested than the other, it should work out just fine. Some of the simplest of tasks like chores can be difficult for people with ADHD to complete, not because they find them physically hard but because they are tedious duties that do not strike any interest in them. It will be very beneficial for the person with ADHD to receive clear instructions regarding priorities and get help completing the most important tasks. Remember, it is very easy for neurodiverse brains to get side-tracked by the less important things if it is interesting to them. Hiring help at home or a professional organizer can help ease the load on the relationship. Most often than not, the issue with a relationship where one of the partners is neurodiverse is misunderstanding and misinterpreting actions and intents. Couple therapy can also be beneficial even though things might not seem to be going bad. It is suggested that this state is avoided altogether, and even if there are no serious or threatening issues you wish to address at any given time, therapy will help you learn effective communication.

Lastly, it is important to never look at the neurodiverse partner and see them as a burden or a duty, but rather think of it as having a partner who is trying to accommodate one's needs, but their condition gets in the way of that. There are ways of overcoming this, and working together is where it all starts.

Chapter 2: ADHD Women and Motivation

Motivation is inconsistent in people with ADHD. When they focus their attention on certain tasks, they manage to complete them easily but struggle to find the spark to start others. From the neurotypical perspective, people who manage to focus on one task should be able to focus on every task in the same way. This can come across as a lack of willpower and just being lazy. This is not a willpower issue but a problem in the chemical dynamics of the brain. The process by which their perception and consciousness change towards things they find interesting is not voluntary. ADHDers can struggle with their working memory for prioritizing duties step by step. Emotions are a powerful and critical aspect of motivation. Emotions play an important role in executive functions like initiation, prioritization, maintaining or shifting interest, holding logic in memory and picking tasks or avoiding them. The brain responds to the intensity of emotions relating to memories. Executive functions are not only driven by conscious feelings but also by unconscious ones. These unconscious emotions cause one to act inconsistently. Usually, this process leads to failure to complete tasks, disengagement from actions altogether, or doubt if a task is completed. Someone with ADHD may want to complete the task and want to give it their full attention; however, they do not manage to act upon it. They will continue to procrastinate and put it off. ADHDers seek distraction and spend their time on less important things.

These are ways people with ADHD can overcome their lack of motivation:

1.   Celebrate small milestones. Try incorporating things that can feel rewarding during the day and give this priority. Make sure you do not just focus on work but also include creative tasks that you enjoy doing. You can make a small list of things you can do to celebrate when you have completed small tasks. Set rewards for when the small tasks are completed so you can have something to look forward to. Try sticking to small but frequent rewards rather than far-fetched ones; otherwise, you can get discouraged.

2.   Remove uncertainty in your life. Try conquering your lack of motivation by sounding more certain in your decisions. Avoid using "should" instead of "must" for things you know you have to do. Try finding the little positive things in the tasks you avoid doing. Although you hate doing the laundry, try keeping in mind that once your laundry baskets are empty and your clothes are organized, you feel accomplished and motivated, and you can't get this feeling unless you do the laundry.

3.   Be creative. If you have been assigned a task or know you have to complete a chore, try to think of creative ways you can complete this task, and if someone else can do it better than you, do not be afraid to assign it to them, in exchange for a task you like doing. If you do not have this luxury, you can always outsource your tasks, like getting a housekeeper every so often to help you clean the house if you dread doing it alone or avoid it altogether.

4.   Customizing tasks according to your interests. If you must complete this task and no one else can do it on your behalf, try to change the process according to your needs. You do not have to complete a task according to what everyone else does or using their methods. These will probably not work for you. If you struggle to complete your grocery list because you get distracted during peak hours, try going later during the day or meet up with a friend and turn this into an outing.

5. Make the process exciting for you. Make sure you treat yourself when you complete the task and try setting a timer if you work better under pressure. If the task feels overwhelming, try planning ahead of time so you can divide it into different milestones. You can find it easier to complete simpler tasks and can reward yourself as you go along.

Make sure you identify what excites and recharges you; otherwise, you will not know what tasks you are willing to complete and those you dread. If you have set limitations for yourself because of past failures, make sure you identify these instances and, if needed, speak to a therapist. Ensure you always know who the second-best option is to complete the task on your behalf and know you need to be willing to exchange tasks. Try recalling a time when you managed to complete the task and identify the differences between then and now. Try bringing back some of those elements into the present situation to help you complete the task or at least find the motivation to start.

If the people around you struggle to understand your motivation and your lack of it in different scenarios, try explaining to them that you experience a disconnection between your intentions and goals. If they think this can simply be hurdled by inspiration, motivation and self-discipline, explain that you may have had instances where you completed this task without issue, but the reason you are struggling now is not laziness. Neurotypical brains can struggle with lengthy, repetitive and boring tasks. Urgent and novel things will strike a motivation in you like no other, especially if it interests you. Working under pressure or with urgency can give you a dopamine kick and get you working on your task. Stimulating and engaging activities are things you know you can complete if you have ADHD.

Seeking stimulation via medication or exercise is not a luxury for people with ADHD but a necessity. If your superiors at work know you have ADHD, you may ask them to create different deadlines before the major one to help you submit minor parts of the project and to help you avoid procrastinating till the very last minute to complete a project. If you are in school, try asking your teacher for mini-deadlines for drafts of your assignment, or otherwise, find a close friend who can keep you accountable. Having someone to answer to can encourage you to keep up with deadlines. If you often feel ashamed to have people over because your house is always a mess, try inviting your friends over, so you are bound to clear the clutter and organize your space for when guests come over.

If you have taken up hobbies, you must understand that whatever feels interesting now may no longer be in a few months, and that is fine. You may have a list of things you enjoy doing, and if you are fed up with some, you can have a list to choose from but know you can always go back to playing that old guitar of yours whenever the motivation is rekindled.

Chapter 3: ADHD Women and Social Skills

Impulsive, disorganized, violent, overly sensitive, intense, emotional, or destructive actions are common perceptions in people with ADHD. Their relationships with others in their social world, parents, siblings, teachers, colleagues, co-workers and spouses or partners, are often marred by confusion and miscommunication. The ability to self-regulate one's behavior and reactions toward others is impaired in people with ADHD. Relationships may become unnecessarily strained and unstable because of this. As a result, people with ADHD often face social challenges, social rejection and interpersonal relationship issues. Emotional pain and suffering are caused by such negative interpersonal outcomes. They tend to play a role in the development of comorbid mood and anxiety disorders as well.

To interact viably with others, an individual should be mindful and ready to control indiscreet practices. Grown-ups with ADHD are frequently unmindful and careless and regularly need reminders to control their behavior. Since ADHD is an "undetectable incapacity," often unnoticed by the individuals who might be new to the problem, socially unseemly practices that are the side effects of ADHD are frequently attributed to different causes. That is, individuals regularly see these practices and the person who submits them as inconsiderate, conceited, untrustworthy, apathetic, uncouth and many other adverse character attributes. Over time, such negative marks lead to the social dismissal of the person with ADHD. Social dismissal causes enthusiastic torment in the existence of many youngsters and grown-ups who have ADHD and can cause destruction and lower confidence levels for the duration of their life. In a relationship, improper social conduct may outrage the companion without ADHD, who may in the long run "wear out" and abandon the relationship or marriage. Educating people with ADHD, significant others and their companions about ADHD and how it influences their social abilities and relational practices can help mitigate a large part of the contention and fault. Simultaneously, the person with ADHD needs to learn procedures to become as capable and conceivable in a social environment, so effort needs to go both ways. With an appropriate appraisal, treatment and training, people with ADHD can figure out how to communicate with others viably such that it improves their public image.

Observing people, copying their actions, practicing and receiving input are common ways to learn social skills. They may grasp what is proper yet come up short in general on social expectations. Shockingly, as grown-ups, they regularly acknowledge "something" is missing yet are never fully sure what that "something" might be. Social acknowledgment can be seen as going up or down. People who show proper social abilities are compensated with more acknowledgment from those they socialize with and are encouraged to utilize their friendly abilities. For those with ADHD, the winding regularly goes the other way. Their absence of social abilities prompts peer dismissal, limiting the freedom to master social skills, which prompts more dismissal, and the cycle goes on. Social discipline incorporates dismissal, evasion and other more obvious methods for displaying one's objection towards someone else. Note that individuals do not frequently tell the offender the reason for the social infringement. Calling attention to a social mistake is frequently considered socially unacceptable. Hence, individuals are almost always left all alone to attempt to improve their social abilities without seeing precisely what aspects need improvement because there is no feedback from others.

Make sure you notice others' body language, tone of voice and behavior. Do not avoid eye contact but rather maintain it. Give enough importance to other people's choice of words as that can translate into what they want to say. For example, if they say they would love to do something, they probably want to do it. Be attentive to actions because they speak louder than words. If you have someone around you that you trust, and they know about your ADHD, try telling them about your perceptions and see if you are on the same page. Do not be afraid to ask for various perspectives from different people. Someone with ADHD can be engaged in a conversation and miss the main point of the conversation. If they ask again to verify or gather what they have missed, they are often perceived as inattentive and missing out on details intentionally, when this is not the case. Repeating information can be frustrating for the other party. People with ADHD can struggle with translating communication adequately enough for them to understand it, let alone reading between the lines. This can pose an issue because what is said is not always what is meant, so ADHDers can often miss the message implied by the other parties.

During an ADHD assessment, the physician takes into consideration the individual's social skills and can ask for a report from the ADHDer and their spouses or partners for confirmation.

These reports can often include the following incidents:

- Paying attention when spoken to is difficult and often misses vital details.

- Appears to be unconcerned with others.

- Taking turns in conversation is difficult.

- Tendency to interrupt frequently.

- Having trouble completing activities or duties.

- Inability to use correct etiquette.

- Misses verbal cues.

- Living an unorganized way of life.

- Shares information inappropriately.

- Find noises or vibrations others can easily shut out distracting.

- Immediately shutting down when feeling swamped or frustrated.

- Thoughts that are disorganized.

- Abruptly ending a discussion.

- Have trouble keeping friends or maintaining relationships.

- Going off-topic during conversations and getting distracted by unrelated thoughts.

- Being unreliable because you give off the vibe of someone who can be counted on, but you fail to meet deadlines.

- Overreacting, lashing out, or having meltdowns when it is not appropriate.

Social skills can be worked upon, and once the flaws are identified, it is important to speak to an ADHD coach or a therapist who can help you better these skills. Medication usually helps with certain impulsive actions and hyperactivity because it allows for more concentration and self-control; however, medications alone cannot provide the sufficient help needed to gain the required skills for socializing. Therapy can often include role-play, modeling, feedback and instructions. There are also ways to improve social skills through changes you apply yourself. Start by gaining knowledge on social skills and identify areas that need improvement. Apply a positive attitude and make sure you are open to growth. Make sure you are open to feedback and take this constructively and not personally. Once you identify your flaws, make sure you take one skill at a time and improve on it as you go. Make sure you master one skill before you move on to the next one. If you are struggling with gathering all the important information in a conversation, try to ask for a repetition of what was said to clarify and make sure you understood everything said without leaving out any major details. If you look up to someone around you and feel like their skills are way developed than yours, use them as a model.

Once you gain these skills, try practicing them via role-playing. Allow the person you are practicing with to provide you with feedback. If you cannot do role-play, you can also try visualizing circumstances under which you can utilize these skills. Try running it through your mind and practice it as much as possible. Make sure that visualizations are realistic and practice the skill in situations and with people you are likely to need it. ADHDers who lack social skills may use prompts to help them stay on track. If you are often fidgety and talk a lot, try setting reminders on your watch every five minutes. People who are honest, loyal, understanding, trustworthy, considerate and reliable are more likely to have social relationships. Try developing these skills, and you will be more likely to create and maintain healthy relationships.

With the help of combined treatment like therapy and medication, if you are already on any, you can learn to stop before you speak your mind and filter any inappropriate information you are about to give to others. Making those around you aware of your ADHD wherever possible can help them understand your intentions if you slip up and avoid misunderstanding you. If you feel like you never fit in or struggle to make new friends, it is because your social skills are lacking due to your ADHD.

While ADHD can make social interactions more difficult, there is knowledge and services available to help you develop your social skills. Get advice from books, therapy, or coaching, and most importantly, make and sustain social ties. You do not need a lot of friends to improve your skills. A small circle of reliable and honest friends is all you need.

Chapter 4: ADHD Women and Social Anxiety

Social anxiety disorder, also known as SAD, is one of the most common anxiety disorders that can coexist with ADHD. In one or more social contexts, social anxiety is correlated with a distinct fear of possibly devastating attention and judgment from others. Worries about embarrassment and rejection are common in people with social anxiety, and they can last for six months or longer. Worrying about being judged negatively by others can limit involvement in events, interests and relationships; it can also make it difficult to form new relationships. It is crucial to understand the nuances between the two conditions when it comes to managing and treating them. Although experts are unsure why ADHD and SAD always coexist, some believe that the same factors that trigger ADHD, like genetics, environmental contaminants, or premature birth, may often exacerbate anxiety disorders. Others agree that the signs of ADHD, in and of themselves, lead to anxiety. Inattention, hyperactivity and impulsivity are common symptoms of ADHD, and they place a person at risk of being ridiculed, mocked, or otherwise socially rejected. Fearing more rejection, many people withdraw into themselves, avoiding any potentially threatening social situations. At first glance, ADHD and SAD may seem the same. If you suffer from SAD, you are constantly concerned about being viewed negatively by others. It might be difficult for you to attend social gatherings. You may be aware that your fear is unfounded, but you feel helpless to change it, as with other anxiety disorders.

The following are some symptoms where ADHD and SAD overlap:

Struggle to socialize—Because people with SAD fear rejection, they struggle to socialize. Likewise, people with ADHD can also struggle to read between the lines and have low control over their impulses resulting in a lack of maintained social relations.

Inattentive—People with ADHD can often come across as inattentive, and that is because their brain affects their focus. People with SAD can also seem inattentive, and that is because their brain is taken over by worrisome thoughts.

Struggle completing tasks—People with SAD often struggle to complete tasks, and those with ADHD also find difficulty sticking to deadlines or plans as they should.

Try these simple steps to start reducing your social anxiety:

Focus on one thing—Begin by looking for quick wins to boost your confidence in yourself and self-esteem. What is the one thing you wish you could change that is causing you the most difficulty right now? Focus on this target repeatedly to summon the will to confront what worries you. Find someone to help you in this process. You'll need someone to hold you accountable, such as a sibling, a relative, a psychiatrist, or a mentor.

Start light—Start small to avoid being discouraged at first. Before taking on a larger mission, master a transition that is within your grasp. For example, if you are shy about meeting new people but want to make new friends, expecting to make 10 friends on your first try might be asking too much of yourself. Instead, consider the first, very small move you might take: ask someone you do not know a question.

Be compassionate with yourself—People who have ADHD and social anxiety tend to be very critical of themselves. For years, you have heard cynical stories about how you have missed the mark and what you should do differently. You continue to unwittingly follow this dialogue over time. Begin by thinking about something inspirational you might say to yourself, "I am smarter than I thought," for example. Write it on Post-it notes, then place them at vantage points within your surroundings. This may sound corny, but you need to know what to say to the cynical voice when it tells you that you can't take a risk to try anything new. Consider keeping a written diary in which you record one daily achievement about your challenge. Go back to it whenever you feel down because you failed one task, and it also helps to keep yourself accountable and on track.

Be mindful—When you are having a panic attack or are caught up in a guilt trip as a result of social anxiety, try to become more conscious of your physical body and your breathing. This is your exit ticket from the spiral. When people are nervous, their breathing picks up as adrenaline takes over. This is our fight-or-flight reaction at work. In these situations, you must ground yourself and slow down your breathing. Try putting one hand on your shoulders and the other on your stomach. Breathe into both hands, feeling their weight, and pretend that you are breathing in a soothing color with each breath. Do this for a few minutes. Alternate nostril breathing from yoga can also be used for five rounds. You can feel uncomfortable and insecure when you work to alleviate your anxiety. Those are indications that you're on the right track.

Talk to someone every day—You must exercise your social skills, even though you do not want to. Combat your natural proclivity toward loneliness by engaging in a 3 to 5-minute interaction with someone outside your home at least three days per week. It can be done via Zoom or FaceTime, over the internet, or in person, but you must make real-time contact with someone who cannot be reached via text messaging or social media. Make a list of people you call: distant or near relatives, cousins, siblings who have passed on, grandparents and so on. You cannot enhance your ability to communicate with others or read their emotional state by email, which is precisely the talent you need to develop. If you are unsure what to say, prepare any questions ahead of time, or ask your accountability partner for assistance and practice. Having a list of people, you know you can go to practice and enhance your skill is much easier than having to think at the top of your head because you are less likely to be encouraged and talk to strangers or to people you do not feel comfortable with.

Anxiety is a formidable opponent that tries to keep you disarmed, so it takes bravery and maturity to face it. To effectively address social anxiety, you must first set a fair and achievable target and be prepared to feel some discomfort along the way. That is how you can learn and develop the skills you need to gain the social trust and relationships you desire. You cannot be able to get rid of all the social anxiety at once.

Chapter 5: ADHD Women and Shaming

hame is something that lots of adult ADHD patients feel, and it can be deafening. The root cause of shame lies mostly in the fact that ADHD patients feel they have not been able to keep up with others' expectations and have been a complete failure throughout their life. If not addressed, the sense of failure can hamper self-esteem and become a very big emotional burden. So, you should never be afraid to go to someone and ask them for help, especially professional help. If you are feeling sorry and perpetually unworthy, then you are also a victim of ADHD shame. It can be a haunting thing to endure for a lifetime. That is why it is of utmost importance that you find out the root cause of your shame, understand why you have to do something about it and then take the necessary steps.

What Is Shame?

Even though it might seem unrealistic, people do misunderstand the concept of shame and mix it up with other feelings. In order to prevent it, first, you must have a comprehensive idea of what shame is. If you are someone struggling with ADHD, then you already know that every day feels like you keep apologizing to others for something or the other. It might be because you didn't do the laundry, didn't clean your desk, were late to the office, or lost your car keys. No matter how hard the ADHD patients try, these things keep happening over and over again.

It eventually leads to a cycle of self-blame, where apologizing for even insignificant things becomes a habit. It happens even more in those patients who were diagnosed with ADHD later in life. Ultimately, these patients are numbed by a sense of shame, and it can be very crippling. Things can go to such an extent where people refrain from looking into their wardrobe because they know it's messy and they are ashamed of it. They feel tortured for every disorganized part of their lives.

So, to put it in simpler terms, shame can be described as a constant state of embarrassment and feeling of inadequacy. The person feels as if he/she is humiliated all the time. In extreme cases, people are no longer the person they really are in front of others, and this gives them a feeling of having a secret life. Out of all the symptoms that ADHD patients have to face, shame is definitely one of the most painful ones and it can easily wreak emotional havoc. The patients keep indulging in negative self-talk and it is more or less like wearing an anvil throughout your life.

Thus, when people experience shame, they are somehow ashamed of a certain part of themselves. They struggle a lot in their daily life, but they don't want others to know about it. So, they put up a façade where they lead a happy life. But with time, this constant need to be someone else brings a feeling of loneliness, and it is exhausting. The patients start withdrawing themselves from their close ones as well, and eventually, they can't seek support from their family members because they are crippled by shame.

There are different types of shame in ADHD, and we are going to discuss them below:

The first type of shame is where the person is simply ashamed of the fact that they have ADHD. They cannot be comfortable with this medical condition. Even though it is a lifelong condition and people have to accept it as if they have different hair colors, it is not so easy.

The next type of shame that ADHD patients feel is that they

are different from others. They look at others and then they look at themselves. They notice significant differences. This shame of not being the same as others is more crippling in children than in adults. Everyone has the desire to fit in, but with ADHD, you will always have differences that will make you stand out in the room (and not in a good way). This constant attention that ADHD patients receive when they walk into a room also gives them social anxiety. But it is not only the behavioral differences that set them apart, ADHD patients often need extra help, and they also have to take meds throughout the day and keep up with their doctor's appointments.

The next type of shame that ADHD patients have is about their behaviors. They do not behave the same as others. They almost always end up doing something where others make them feel embarrassed. They feel embarrassed because their work desk or their home is not as tidy and clean as that of others. Every person is affected differently when it comes to behavioral shame. But all of them have one thing in common—they are ashamed.

Another common type of shame noticed in ADHD adults is that they are not satisfied with their position in life and they feel that they did not put in enough effort. They had set certain goals and they feel like they haven't reached those milestones. The shame from this feeling is worsened when they see others around them doing great things while they can't. This also causes resentment because ADHD adults are just as smart as the others, and yet they have drawbacks.

ADHD patients keep ruminating about their pasts and they bring up every instance in their minds where they failed at doing something. It can be the time they missed paying their credit card bill or the time when they had to break up with someone special. It can also be the most embarrassing moment of their life. They keep playing it over and over again and they relive that shame from time to time.

You should also understand that shame and guilt are two very different things. You feel guilty about what you have done but you feel ashamed of who you are as a person.

Chapter 6: ADHD Women and Driving

People with ADHD have been known to become distracted easily and take risks whilst driving. This is because the executive functions and working memory play a large role in driving and there is a level of impulsivity and disorganization outside driving. People with ADHD lack self-awareness and awareness of others. They accelerate and brake too quickly causing them to take risks. This brings risk to themselves and the other people on the road. They are not able to stay focused on the task at hand. Preventing accidents is important, especially when ADHD women are involved because there is an increased "crash risk."

When taking an examination, people with ADHD often magnify the task in order to complete the task in their typical way. This can be in relation to their inattention, inattentive blindness, the inattentive processing style and their delay in switching.

Why Drivers with ADHD May Be at Increased Risk?

There are many reasons people with ADHD are at an increased risk of getting into car crashes. They do not think clearly about the risks involved in what they are doing. The ADHD brain cannot keep up with the speed at which the person is living their life. They are unorganized and distracted. They take risks and do not think clearly about the dangers involved. You may think that there are other factors that cause an increased risk of crashes for drivers with ADHD. They are also less able to reduce their speed due to their inability to use self-management. They are impatient, restless, impulsive and easily distracted, all of which can cause them to crash on the road.

Symptoms of ADHD Women Examined

Some of the problems people with ADHD sufferers may face on the road. Impulsivity results in the inability to resist the urge to act immediately. They often act rashly on their impulse. Connectivity Problems may result in knowing what you should do but do not know how to do it. There may be problems with linking cause to effects. Following directions may be difficult because of inattention, lack of perception of detail, carelessness, inability to focus on the main point, or tendency to get stuck on irrelevant details or visual-spatial problems. They also get distracted and may get too involved in an activity for it to be classified as distractible. They may let others organize and plan for them and simply go along with whatever is suggested. It often appears that they cannot get things done and the dependents can get into a lot of trouble.

The deficit in Meta-Cognition means that they do not know what is going on around them very much. The more impulsive they are, the more likely they are to get confused about what is going on around them. Their perception is poor and they cannot read the world around them very well. They may have a very difficult time seeing how they themselves fit into a bigger picture. They have a poor sense of time and they do not have a good idea of either where they are going or how long they have been going there. They have a problem with setting their own goal and they do not understand why they should set goals. Their self-image is vague and they do not need to satisfy their own needs even though they desperately do. They do better when someone takes care of them. In general, their problems with planning and organization cause them to participate less in society as a whole. The ability to engage in self-observation and self-consciousness is difficult for them. They have increased use of reasoning as opposed to feelings or gut feelings. They have a decreased ability to understand what they cannot see.

Chapter 7: ADHD Women and Sleep Problems

O ver half of adults with ADHD report going to bed late and waking up late. They also confess to having trouble with feeling tired after a night of sleep during the day if they do not wake up late. They rarely manage to fall asleep effortlessly or wake up feeling good in the morning.

The physical and mental restlessness in adults with ADHD disrupts a person's sleep, leaving them with exhaustion. The reason why there was never a direct link between sleep issues and ADHD is that this was not strongly evident in kids with ADHD but became more consistently present in adults with ADHD. To date, sleep disturbances are considered as coexisting issues of ADHD and medication used to treat ADHD may have been accused of interfering with healthy sleeping patterns in people with ADHD. Sufferers call this perverse sleep, which pretty much works in reverse; they are awake when they want to be asleep and fall asleep when they want to stay awake. This is also known as delayed sleep phase syndrome. People with ADHD tend to have trouble with their circadian rhythm, sometimes also referred to as the internal clock. This regulates sleep and wake patterns.

A lot of people with ADHD report restlessness, specifically at night. They describe it as their mind racing as soon as they decide to fall asleep, leaving them unable to sleep at night. They might also describe themselves as night owls and tend to work better at night. They would not be morning persons and completing the simplest of tasks in the morning can prove to be extremely challenging. Some also report taking over an hour trying to fall asleep at night. When people with ADHD manage to fall asleep, they often toss and turn a lot and are very sensitive to noises around them. They wake up to the slightest sound, which mostly reduces the hours and quality of sleep, having them wake up in the morning as tired as they went to bed the night before. People with ADHD often wake up multiple times during the night, and when they manage to get into a deep sleep, they find it very hard to wake up in the morning. They will eventually wake but do so groggily and may need a huge cup of coffee to kickstart the brain.

It is suggested that improved sleep hygiene is applied. This will foster and initiate the sleep process and hopefully maintain it. Sleep hygiene can vary according to the individual. Ideally, and as a standard, the bed should be kept as a place for sleep and intimate action, not to argue or to work. You must have a set bedtime routine and many phone applications can help you do this. It would be beneficial to consider avoiding naps during the day. If you require specific sounds or music, make sure you have it set up by the time you go to bed. Warm showers or baths can help you get sleepier. If some sounds bother you at night or hinder your sleep, try your best to eliminate them, and try wearing earplugs to block out noise. If you want to try and go to sleep, try getting into bed, to begin with. Avoid drinking coffee late at night because we all know caffeine will keep you awake and because it is a diuretic, it will also wake you up several times during the night for multiple visits to the bathroom. Ideally, consumption of any liquids is minimalized closer to bedtime and gadgets like your tablet or laptop should be put down 2 to 3 hours before bedtime as the blue light they emit will hinder the production of melatonin, making you unable to fall asleep. If you must work late at night, try using a blue light filter to avoid disrupting your sleep. Some spectacles can come with this filter even if you do not have to wear prescription glasses, so the lens serves purely as a blue light filter. Certain foods are also said to help and promote sleep, such as kiwis, nuts, tart cherries juice and grapes. Valerian and chamomile teas also help. Meditating 10 to 15 minutes before bedtime can help you relax.

There are plenty of things one can do to promote a healthier sleeping pattern, but it starts by giving your symptoms the diagnosis and importance they deserve. If your ADHD is overlooked, you will, in return, receive inadequate treatment.

Chapter 8: ADHD Women and Emotional Dysregulation

If you have ADHD and find yourself on an emotional rollercoaster, it is probably caused by your emotional dysregulation. This is a big part of how ADHD affects the lives of neurodiverse individuals. Some doctors do not consider emotional dysregulation as one of the symptoms of ADHD because the literature they use to help identify people with ADHD does not list emotional dysregulation as being part of them. Researchers wanted to measure results that could be assessed in a laboratory, but emotions are a bit hard to compute like that. Research is, all the time, evolving and there is an understanding of emotional dysregulation and its prominence in ADHD.

Emotional dysregulation can get in the way of one's goals and may make someone with ADHD not so fun to be around in certain situations if, for example, those around them do not understand their condition and their intentions. Emotional dysregulation will not always exhibit itself in the same way in different situations. It might help to keep track of your emotions and jot down how you feel in certain situations. This can help you identify your bad habits, and by being more aware of them, you can learn to avoid getting into these habits in the first place. In this way, you can understand better when your emotions are getting you in trouble or hindering your goals. Awareness is also where to start. Being aware of your emotions will help you slow down your emotional reactions leaving time for you to think and decide how you want to respond instead of reacting impulsively. This is also called mindfulness and is a method of meditation. It will make you more aware of your thoughts and interpret them without judgment. You must be curious to explore ways to deal with these emotions to the best of your abilities. This will help to reduce stress overall.

Not everyone suffering from ADHD will experience emotional dysregulation, but those who do will often describe themselves as very emotional. Borderline personality disorder or mood disorder can also have emotional dysregulation as a symptom. This is also why people with ADHD, specifically women, may get misdiagnosed. People with emotional dysregulation can be sensitive to criticism, have perceived rejections and be overly sensitive to teasing. They would often find it hard to brush of teasing comments from those around them and would take it very seriously. Emotional responses in people with emotional dysregulation are often displayed as emotional responses at a higher magnitude than those without this issue. It would be beneficial to let the people around you know what you are overly sensitive about and the jokes or teasing comments you would not tolerate. Those that care and understand you will do their best to avoid passing comments on things they know will upset you. People with emotional dysregulation often seem impatient, tense and edgy. This would not necessarily mean someone finds it hard to sit still through a meeting or finds it hard to relax. It is more like extreme levels of frustration internally. For example, if technological devices, such as laptops or mobile phones, are faulty, you are likely to get frustrated because you need them to work. If something is not going to plan, it may also trigger emotional dysregulation and one may find it hard to assess the situation in a practical way, detached from one's emotions.

Mood swings are also another symptom of emotional dysregulation. You may wake up in a negative mood only to end the day with a positive feeling. It might be difficult to deal with the negative moments in your life, but you must remember that nothing is permanent and that this too shall pass. You might feel negative about yourself because you had a target to reach, which you failed to do by mid-day but by the end of the day, something may happen that will turn your mood around. If you reflect on the past and realize that you've been in this situation before and recall how it ended, you will realize you are going to get through it. People with emotional dysregulation may also experience emotional outbursts. It may not always be the case for people with emotional dysregulation because some may bottle up their emotions leading to internal frustration rather than exerting their anger.

Lastly, people with emotional dysregulation can have a harder time going back to a neutral emotional baseline, and it will take them longer to get back to their calmer state. This can be highly impacted by the people you surround yourself with. If those around you have fluctuating emotions as well, it will leave you feeling uneasy, and because you are anxious and constantly on the lookout for when the other shoe will drop, you have a tough time feeling at ease around them. It is important who you surround yourself with because, from teasing and jokes to the positive or negative vibes they emit, it will all affect your emotions and how you feel towards those emotions. If you are surrounded by someone who makes you feel at ease, safe and fully understands your flaws, they are more likely to understand your intentions and will be less likely to trigger or set your emotional dysregulation issue off even over frivolous things. On the other hand, if you are ringed by negative people whose emotions are even more alternating than yours, you are very likely to be anxious around them.

Emotional dysregulation can have its positive sides. People with ADHD can enjoy feeling strong emotions and are usually very sensitive to the emotions others around them experience, making them very empathetic. They easily get excited and are not able to hide that excitement. This makes people with ADHD very fun to be around. This makes them very interesting, passionate and expressive people. Emotions are a way of communicating with ourselves and others too. They can also motivate new ventures, like when you are excited about an idea which you finally start working on and turn into a new project or business. A healthy diet with the right water intake coupled with the right amount of sleep will help make you feel less edgy and irritable. Physical activity will relieve stress, depression, anxiety and symptoms of ADHD. Because physical activity increases endorphin release in the body, it will boost your overall mood. Regular short 10-minute walks can do magic for your mood. Meditation or yoga sessions can also help you relax. If you notice that caffeine or a high sugar intake makes you feel jittery or anxious, avoid them altogether. It is important to get help if you are experiencing emotional dysregulation because it often leads to problems in relationships and at work. It may lead to anxiety and depression. You may lean towards substance abuse to help cope with your emotions if this is left untreated. Cognitive behavior therapy can be very beneficial for people who experience emotional dysregulation as part of their ADHD and is usually given by therapists.

Chapter 9: ADHD Women and Sexuality

ADHD in adult women already impacts their lives, including difficulty maintaining stable relationships and fostering a poor self-image. Symptoms affecting sexuality can vary from person to person and may be hard to measure for this reason. Common ADHD symptoms can include emotional instability, depression and anxiety. All of these can harm your sex drive. If you are constantly focusing your time and energy on staying organized, you will probably not have much energy left to get involved in sexual activities with your partner.

Two commonly reported symptoms of ADHD and sexuality are hypersexuality and hyposexuality. Although sexual dysfunction is not one of the diagnostic criteria for ADHD, it is still very much real. Hypersexuality refers to an uncommonly high sex drive. Sexual stimulation releases endorphins in the brain, giving a feeling of calmness and reducing restlessness — two very common feelings in people with ADHD. ADHD individuals are already probably very impulsive, and this may have them engage in risky sexual behavior. People with ADHD may also experience hyposexuality, where their sex drive drops. This may be due to the condition itself or caused by medications used to treat ADHD. The same issues people with ADHD face during normal day-to-day activities will also be faced during sex. They will have a hard time concentrating, may lose interest and become distracted.

Women with ADHD may have trouble achieving orgasm because they either reach it too quickly or not at all despite lengthy stimulations. People with ADHD may be hypersensitive, meaning they have extreme physical sensitivity. What may feel good to the non-ADHD partner may feel irritating to the ADHD sufferer. Odors, touch and tastes often involved in sex may come across as nasty to someone with ADHD. Getting intimate in the first place can also be a challenge for people with ADHD because of their hyperactivity. They may struggle to relax enough to set the mood for sex. Neurodiverse brains are mostly always busy, and when their brain is focused on a million other things, it is very hard to transition into sex. ADHD individuals tend to get distracted during sex, particularly women, but even neurotypical brains do this. It is possible for people with ADHD to hold their focus throughout sex but initiating activity can be a challenge. ADHD brains tend to rate higher on sexual eagerness because they are more willing to try new things and may contribute to keeping things more exciting in the bedroom. This does not mean that all ADHD individuals experience sexuality the same way because everyone is different.

Surprisingly enough, ADHD and its effects on sexuality are not solely about sex itself but more about how ADHD is managed, either by ADHD brains or their partners. Whoever tries hard enough to manage their ADHD and makes sure their partners know they are trying will more likely experience intimacy when compared to those that do not put in the effort. Making the other party aware of your efforts is very important. It is easy to see that you are trying hard enough or putting in the effort because you are very aware of your actions. It will be a little harder knowing what your partner is doing because you cannot see it all. If awareness is not present, it will be easy to have one of the partners, usually, the neurotypical one, feel like they work harder or put in more effort than their other half, usually the ADHDer. Putting in the effort the other party expects can be a good start, although the effort might not mean everything is as your partner expects it to be.

They are more likely to appreciate your good intentions even though not everything is as they please. If they walk into the living room only to find a mess but know that it is you trying, they are more likely to feel happier towards you because they know you are doing the best you can. The neurotypical brain would feel that although their needs are not being met fully, there is an effort, and the intention is to try. If there is not enough communication and the non-ADHD partner does not recognize that their ADHD counterparts are putting in the effort, it may be demoralizing for the ADHDer. They may come across as careless when, in fact, they do care. If their effort goes unnoticed, they may be inclined to give up rather than try their best. ADHD needs to be managed by the partner suffering from it and by the neurodiverse partner.

If you take ADHD more seriously and put in the effort to manage the condition, you are more likely to remember your duties in the relationship and complete more and more of them. This will result in more harmony in the relationship where both parties feel their needs are being met or mostly met. With the right setup, couples will want to have sex with each other. If the non-ADHD partner feels like their needs are being overlooked, they are more likely to complain about it as they would feel like they are putting in all the effort and they are alone. The ADHD partner will likely get defensive, discouraged and try minimizing the gravity of the situation. On the inside, the ADHD partner would still feel that whatever it is that they are doing is not enough and is constantly failing. Non-ADHD partners may expect their ADHD partners to do things and complete tasks as a neurotypical brain would, but this is not possible for neurodiverse individuals. A partner that challenges you to bring out the best in yourself is the ideal partner. With that said, it is important that no one in the relationship feels like they are selling out their integrity and compromising more than they should. It should not be like you are doing too much for someone else but not enough for yourself. It is important to never get the feeling of someone doing too much and the other half not doing enough. A balance needs to be achieved so no one feels like they are either selfish or being used.

It can be ideal if, with compromise, couples chose to try new techniques to reduce the risk of boredom during sex. It is very important to be attentive and sensitive to the other person's feelings and goals. Any plans need to be approved by both partners. It is best to communicate and discuss how ADHD affects your intimacy. Partners need to be considerate to each other's needs and adjust accordingly. If perfumes or light bother the partner with ADHD, then agree to avoid these triggers altogether in the bedroom. Sex therapy or couple therapy can also be beneficial. Doing calming exercises before the act can help get you both in the mood, like yoga and meditation. Try getting rid of distractions and make plans for intimacy and commit to them. It may not necessarily mean you will get intimate every time, but it will help to have the time set for what is important for both of you and mentally prepare you for what may happen next. Leaving room for transitioning will also help set the mood and get ADHD partners ready for their next task rather than remaining hooked on the previous task they were doing. It will be helpful to expand the definition of sex, and although you want to get intimate today, it does not necessarily mean you will do everything you usually do.

Ultimately ADHD needs to be managed if it is affecting your sex life and your life in general. ADHD cannot be looked at as being the whole story and the big problem. Both partners have their parts to play. ADHD does not create new issues; it just exacerbates universal struggles that even non-ADHD couples have to go through. You may define sex in whatever way works for you, but if it is a priority for the both of you, make time for it. Although you may struggle with getting things started, you will generally feel happy afterward.

Chapter 10: ADHD Women and Money Management

Money management can be an issue for people with ADHD. ADHDers tend to procrastinate, be disorganized and impulsive when it comes to their finances. Sorting out paperwork such as bills and rent notifications can be a burden for people with ADHD. So much so they keep on putting it off until there is no way to avoid it anymore. Financial struggle can have negative implications on people and relationships. This is the number one cause of conflict amongst couples, whether one of the partners has ADHD or not. You must have been accused of impulse spending because of that last-minute decision to buy something that caught your eye in a supermarket window or something more expensive that you thought was worth the splurge. An impulse buy can be as small as a pack of gum or as big as a laptop. Holding impulse spending in check as an adult with ADHD can be difficult, but your bank account and budget will thank you for taking the time to manage your finances and limit impulse buys.

If you have ADHD, you often lose money and time because you are disorganized; remember, time is money. If you live in a country where you are responsible for filing your tax returns, you might struggle to submit these on time. You may misplace receipts or even lose them because you do not have a practical filing system in place. If you find yourself turning to close friends and family to borrow money to cover your debts, you have a money management problem. If you find yourself buying things unnecessarily without considering your set budget and the necessity of these things, it is because of your impulsivity. If you struggle with money management and also happen to have your own business, you might be at risk of filing for bankruptcy. You may pay interest often because you do not make it on time to settle your dues. If you struggle to manage your finances in real-time, it is likely you haven't started planning for your retirement yet. If you are a mother with ADHD, you may struggle with keeping a family budget. It has been proven that stress and sadness can cause overspending. If you are familiar with the above situations, it is time you start to get ahold of your finances and find better ways to manage them.

Tips to improve your money management skills:

• Start by organizing any incoming mail. Sort your bills separately from other correspondence and put your bills where you can see them. This way, you don't lose or forget about them.

• Create a filing system if you still receive bills in the traditional way. Create separate folders and categorize them: home insurance, health insurance, motor insurance, credit card and so on. Make sure you file every bill immediately as you receive it once it is settled. If you have not paid it out yet, leave it at the same spot where you can see it is still pending.

• Create a workstation where you keep all your files, calculator, checkbook and so on. This can help you stop looking for things when you need them, and you know where everything you need to keep your finances organized is.

• Create rules for keeping paperwork. Make sure you keep receipts for the stipulated time as instructed by law in your country or for as long as you need them. Avoid keeping unnecessary paperwork as this will add to your clutter.

• Try to minimize the use of credit cards. Paying with credit cards can give you an unrealistic notion of how much you are spending. Wherever possible, try withdrawing cash as per your budget and try sticking to that. Having cash at hand can help you manage your spending because you can see how much you have left to spend.

- Keep a record of your earning and spending. Create a table on your laptop or a piece of paper and list down all your expenses; ideally, you do this monthly.

- Create a budget taking into consideration your income. Dedicate some of your money for leisure activities and impulse buying but be realistic. Allow time to review your spending at the end of the month. You can write down what you spend at the end of the month and compare it with what you have planned to. This means you can eliminate unnecessary purchases and do better the following month.

- Identify your main categories that require budgeting, for example, fuel, parking, groceries, bills and so on.

- Try to plan by making budgets for months or years to come based on your income. This way you can be realistic about the money you have to spend, especially if you are considering spending more on occasions like holidays or getting new items like buying a new car.

- Try creating direct debits with your bank. You can use this to get a small portion of your salary at the end of the month into a savings account. You can do the same for separate accounts dedicated to paying bills. For example, if you pay your motor insurance once a year but can add up to $600.00 yearly, try dividing that amount by 12, the number of months, and reserve a small portion every month. This way, when your bill arrives, you do not have to reserve the entire amount just to pay this bill from one month's salary. You can end up struggling to make ends meet that month because you did not plan ahead of time. You can do the same for home insurance, condominium expenses, life insurances and so on. Do not be afraid to use technology to help you budget.

- To reduce impulse buys, try leaving your credit cards at

home and only take the set budget in cash with you. Credit cards instigate impulse buying and make it harder to save money. When buying things online, try putting them on your debit card instead. If you made a large purchase on your credit card, get into the habit of writing a check to your bank immediately, so you know you have that purchase covered and already paid off.

• Try putting a sticky note on your credit card with your main goal or what you are saving for written on it. So that every time you grab the card to make an impulse buy, you can have a constant reminder.

If you feel like you are tempted mostly when you get ads online, use certain mobile applications, or go to specific stores, try avoiding your temptations. Remove these apps from your phone and set targets for impulse buys. If you are at a store, try to set a budget; for example, if something is less than $5.00, you can buy it, but if it is more than $100.00, take note of it and go back to the store after a 24-hour time period. If you still think you need that thing, try taking into consideration your set budget for the month, where and how you can use it, and whether you really need it. Try thinking about how often you plan to use it and if you have something already that can perform the same function. If you did not plan for this in this month's budget, then make room for it in next month's if you still feel you need it.

• When shopping, make a list and stick to it.

• You may want to take a calculator with you to the supermarket to total everything you have in your cart before getting to the cashier. You may use the calculator on your phone.

• Do not be intimidated to negotiate your car insurance or mortgage. Shop around for competitive prices.

• As a woman with ADHD who is often struggling with money management, if you feel your partner can do a better job of this, do not be afraid to hand this duty to him or her. You are not failing yourself and your family by doing so. On the contrary, you are safeguarding your family's finances.

- If you struggle to plan your finances yourself, you may want to consider hiring a professional financial planner or coach to help you with this. Allow money for their professional fee in your budget.

- If you are subscribed to online email lists, unsubscribe. Those emails you get in your inbox certainly do not help your impulse buying. They will have you surf the website to buy what you probably do not need or can go without.

- If you tend to get into expensive hobbies like video gaming, find new inexpensive or less expensive hobbies. Try exploring museums with free entrances, join clubs, explore public parks, get into an exercise routine and attend public libraries regularly. If you love reading, but you can never stop buying books all the time and are running out of space. Try borrowing books from a library if you probably read a book once and never return to it again. This can save you money and help declutter your space. Try buying books you want to keep a hard copy of or the ones you are likely to want to read more than once.

- If you and your partner wish to control your spending, try keeping separate bank accounts. If your partner is highly organized, it may cause a conflict if you forget to record checks or fall for an impulse buy.

- If you struggle to create or come up with a detailed budget, try a simple one. That is better than nothing. Try rounding up numbers and budgets in the simplest way possible. If you feel like you can manage your budget if you write things down, then draft a table and simply budget.

- Identify the areas where you struggle the most, be it falling for impulse buys, having bouncing checks, or missing paying bills.

- Identify your goals. Whether you want to save for a car or pay off your credit card debt, it is important to identify your goals; otherwise, you cannot work towards achieving them. Once you have a clear picture of what you want to achieve, you can then figure out how to reach them.

- Try to create a safety net, and when budgeting, try spending less than what you earn. Try transferring a certain amount of money into a savings account straight away. If you can afford and still have money to spare, create an emergency account. If you get a fine or your car breaks down, you do not have to eat out of your savings account. There can be times when this emergency account is not used, and that can be further transferred into your savings account.

- Budget your spending based on your income. If you just started your career, allow yourself time to take off and accept the fact that you might not be making enough money to live a champagne lifestyle just yet. Be realistic about your goals.

Chapter 11: ADHD Women and Time Management

Y ou are not alone if you struggle to manage your time or follow through with your plans. Many individuals with ADHD discover that a combination of inadequate leadership abilities, poor time control and difficulties with working memory results in wasted time and unfinished tasks and schedules at work and at home. Adults' women with ADHD have a different perspective on time. The failure to predict potential incentives and repercussions, as well as the impressive propensity to procrastinate and disregard the static surroundings, all add to the difficulties with schedules, punctuality and preparation. Individuals with ADHD have the most misery and difficulty getting things done while struggling with time management. The advantage of completing tomorrow's tasks or establishing good work routines now could be the avoidance of complications and indisposition later. Understanding and managing ADHD can change if you consider it to be a matter of time management.

Planning and marking time can be two skills people with ADHD lack. Overcoming this hurdle can mean you need to plan your day every day. Try adopting methods that work to your liking. Use external factors to get a realistic idea of time. Try not to over-schedule. People with ADHD tend to be people-pleasers and often avoid refusing requests from people or saying no. This can overburden their schedule with no time left for them to relax. Over-planning can set someone up for failure and frustration.

There are various ways to avoid this, so try the following:

- Get hold of a planner that works for you. Consider

technology, compatibility, aesthetics and ease of usage.

• Once you have a planner, block your schedule with things you know you have to do, like attend work, medical appointments and family dinners. Scheduling activities allows you to see if your day is filled up, which can help you from overcommitting. Rather than making a list of things to do, block out time for each task. If conditions change or something isn't done, it's no huge deal to shift it to another time slot on the calendar. You can see the big picture: the amount of time you have in the day and the things that are starting to take up the time.

• Chose high-priority things to put on your to-do list and jot them down on your planner. Do not overload your day and be realistic on how much a task can take you to complete.

• If you find yourself surfing the internet more often than you should, try switching off auto-play mode and switching of electronic devices or TVs to help you go to sleep earlier.

• Try to schedule regular check-ins with someone you trust so they can help you stay up-to-date on your time management skills.

• Make your lifestyle a priority. Plan for grocery shopping, meal prep and exercise during your day.

• Establish a bedtime and a wake-up time to help motivate you to go to bed and get up in the morning.

Leaving the house on time can often be a challenge for people with ADHD. Think of the time you need to make it on time and allow time to get yourself ready and get there. Leave a time window for emergencies or unforeseeable situations like traffic. Establish a station close to your door at home and hold all important things there, your phone, wallet, glasses and keys. Get ready the night before, prepare clothes, bags, or any items you might need. If you have a false sense of time, which most people with ADHD do, try setting timers for everything you do in the morning to limit the time you spend for every activity like having coffee or taking a shower. Alternatively, you may want to set your time some minutes ahead to ensure you are not late. Allow time for a shower and getting ready, and when your timer goes off, move on; otherwise, you will be late. If you think you can stop by a drive-through coffee shop on your way to work, you probably will be late for work again. So, avoid saying you have one last thing to do because that thing can put you behind schedule, a schedule you worked so hard on planning. Take into consideration the time it took you to complete the same task the last time you did it. If you planned for 30 minutes last time but ended up using twice that amount of time, do not repeat the same mistake this time.

Take into consideration time-eaters, those little things that waste your time, but you often do not consider. These can be walking to work from the tube station, getting out of the parking lot, small talk with passers-by and waiting at elevators. Some people with ADHD end up being late most of the time because they want to avoid getting there early. That can put them in an awkward position and uncomfortable situations. Try leaving things in your car that can help you fill the time if you arrive early, like playing on your phone or reading a magazine. If you always put off cleaning your wallet or your purse, use this time to do so.

Many with ADHD are strongly affected by their surroundings; those without find it easier to ignore environmental stimuli. Neurotypicals may use their executive functions to make decisions based on their interests. The further away from a possible incentive or penalty, the less inspired people with ADHD are by it. On Monday, a Friday deadline means little. A set alarm clock for 6 am does not mean people with ADHD get in bed at 10 pm. If performing a task takes longer, people with ADHD may put it off because the reward is farfetched.

Similarly, if the deadline is not in the coming hours, they are very likely to keep putting off working on that project because they are not encouraged by deadlines or penalties. Many people with ADHD are unaware of potential events and implications as they do not appear on their internal radars until much later, and if a mission is on their agenda, they cannot complete it. This makes them too reliant on the burden of the approaching deadline and, as a result, free to procrastinate. And if they are aware that they should begin sooner, they do not feel the burden fast enough. Meanwhile, the present's temptations build an unequal battle, and the future has a difficult time winning. The more clearly you can recall past emotions and outcomes, the more motivated you can be to make changes in the future.

You can find yourself arriving on time, if not early, and feel much more comfortable and content the next time you use these tips. Time management may seem to be a hazy, alien phenomenon, but it boils down to a tug of war between maximizing the current benefits and maximizing the prospects. Time is money; being late costs you money, so think of the things you can do with that lost money and you can soon be on the way to better managing your time.

Chapter 12: ADHD Women and Organization (At Home & At Work)

Many adult women can struggle with clutter in both the home and the workplace, leaving them feeling exhausted or trapped. Getting coordinated will benefit you in various ways, including increasing efficiency, reducing fear, giving up time wasted searching for stuff and serving as a good role model for your children

Getting tasks underway is one of the most difficult aspects of making a transition. Reward systems or promotions will assist you in being more prepared. Until you begin an organizational project, decide on a prize for yourself after you've completed it. When you've finished the job, make sure to reward yourself. Having a friend assist you will make the job simpler and quicker, especially if you need to declutter. Friends will assist you with getting rid of items because they do not have the same emotional connection to them as you do. You may also find social help in online chat communities. Some have features where you make clear promises to arrange a room, then leave your computer to organize for a while before returning to support each other. You may benefit from using a timer or music. The timer can be programmed to go off in 15-minute intervals, with 15-minute breaks in between. Breaking down a difficult task into simpler steps and tackling these steps one at a time is the only way to master it.

Try the following steps to organize a physical space:

1.   Choose the spaces to be organized. Make a list of the areas you want to declutter.

2.   Arrange them in descending order of difficulty. You may write these down on post-its and stick them to your refrigerator or on the notice board in your study. Estimate how long each task can take you to complete. Once you establish how long it can take you, try dividing that time into smaller intervals with short breaks in between. Do not pretend to clear a whole room in 3 hours without having a break. You can be headed for failure if you do. Dividing the task into realistic intervals can get you a higher rate of success, and as you might have figured by now, starting is a big hurdle for people with ADHD. Once you start off performing the task, you feel a sense of accomplishment which convinces you to persevere and complete it as planned.

3.   Begin with the simplest space. Starting easy can maximize your chances of completing the task and being successful. Because people with ADHD feed off adrenaline rush and stimulation, succeeding at one task can make you more likely to complete the following ones. Divide the room into parts and focus on one at a time, arranging, discarding, or reorganizing each item in that section until it is completed. Dividing the space, you want to organize into quarters can be very helpful. You can plan to declutter a quarter of the room in 30 minutes, for example. This can give you a more realistic notion of time and its management. People with ADHD can struggle with this attribute because they have a false sense of time. When organizing your room, try to keep things according to their function. Keep things where you know you use them and can find them later. If you need cleaning supplies or other things to organize your space, make sure to prepare it before starting on the task. If you need garbage bags or vacuum cleaners, make sure you have them available; otherwise, it can be very easy to get distracted. When clearing your space, decide whether you can get rid of some things, box them, store them away, or keep them handy.

4.   Choose an incentive or inspiration to promote the

completion of this task. Once you complete the task, make sure you reward yourself.

5.   When the smallest room is arranged, work your way up to the most complex, repeating steps if necessary.

Another challenge can be staying organized and maintaining the hard work you have just done. If you work with paper, recycle or trash unnecessary ones. If you can, try working electronically and limit the paper piles. Try using a scanner or an application on your phone to save soft copies of important documents. Create a filing system. Make sure you file every day if possible or as frequently as required to avoid cluttering your space again.

You can create storage space if your area is limited. If you work from your room, try storing work material under your bed or use over-the-door organizers to store smaller things like stationery and pantry items. These would usually hang on the side of a cabinet or a door and help to create storage space. They are usually made either of fabric or plastic and can be bought from your local store for cheap. Besides creating storage space, they also organize your space and help you put things in one spot. Store things where you are likely to spot them easily when needed. This can save you time and frustration.

Try these tips for staying organized and limiting the clutter:

•   If whilst you clean, you end up discovering long-lost items and do not know where they go, collect them in a box and after you are done cleaning, try finding them adequate space.

•   Work at the moment by putting things away immediately when you realize they are out of order. If you walk by an open drawer, close it. If your wastebin is full, empty it. If you see clothes lying around on the floor, pick them up and put them in the laundry basket straight away. If you notice some papers lying around, file them.

- Take ten minutes from your day to clean up around the house. This small step every day can alleviate the burden of having to devote bigger chunks of your day just to clean up your space.

- The most difficult part is getting started, but once you start and see that you are making gains, you are more inclined to stick with it. Try to adopt a mindset that allows you to believe you will only stick to this task for a stipulated amount of time. Once you start, you are more likely to continue.

- Try eliminating an item before you get a new one. After contemplating whether you can get that item, try eliminating something else that you are not using that much or at all. You may donate items you no longer use or resell them. You may want to keep a box on the side for things you no longer need, and once you have enough items, you can make one trip to the charity shop and donate.

After reading these tips, some readers would be able to begin planning. Others can require the help of a mentor, experienced organizer, or therapist to get started. If you need assistance, do not despair or give up. It took a lifetime to get to the state of disarray in which you have been living; it could take years to repair it. The important thing is to get started.

Chapter 13: How to Stop Losing Things

People with ADHD constantly lose or misplace things. This is because you are distracted when putting things away and cannot recollect the last place you left them. You may put things down for what seems to be a split of a second and forget about where you left it. When looking for that thing you just misplaced, you are very likely to get distracted by external stimuli, like the sound coming from your TV set or that open videogame on your laptop. You can empty the dishwasher and do a full load of laundry before remembering to start looking for that thing you lost 2 hours ago. This can cause most people with ADHD to be often late to work or a meeting with friends. Some people with ADHD tend to compensate for this inner turmoil and end up being extremely organized, almost perceived as obsessive-compulsive, but not every ADHD brain is like this.

Try having a dedicated place for everything you use. This strategy can work for the neurotypical brain without struggle, but for an ADHD brain, you might need to modify it a bit to make it suitable for your needs. Putting things away where they mostly make sense does not always work. Something can make sense to be placed somewhere in particular now, but this may not come to mind when you are looking for it. Try placing things where they are most useful. Think of a restaurant or a coffee bar. Every server would have their station, which is always replenished. Those people in a restaurant are the external stimuli people with ADHD struggle to block out. If you take an umbrella with you before leaving the house, try leaving an umbrella holder near the door. If you often leave your jacket everywhere but where it needs to be, try having a coat hanger next to the door. If you often misplace your keys, try installing a key holder next to your door. Your keys can have multiple points of usage because you can place them in your car, bag, or house. Keep those places to a minimum to avoid confusion whenever you need to go look for them. It is perfectly fine to have duplicates or more copies of one item around the house. Take your phone charger as an example. You will probably need one in the bedroom, one in the living room and another at your desk. That is fine. You will avoid looking for it every time you need to charge your phone.

Make it easy to put things back because you know you can struggle with this. You can make use of a label machine to label where things go. This can make it easier for you to put things back, and you do not have to remember where everything is meant to go. Placing things in clear containers can help you know what is in them without having to hover down every canister in your house. Make things fun to put back. Decorate your space and make sure you can easily get acquainted with where things should go. Think of it as if it is a puzzle. Have a look around you and you can probably notice things that are out of place. Take some time to put them back. This can help you keep a decluttered space every day without having a backlog of lost and misplaced items. It can also help you find things easily whenever you need them. Try this with your workstation as well. Try decluttering it every day at the end of your shift. This can help you start the next morning on a good note. Do the same thing with your dishes; try putting dirty dishes in the dishwasher if you have one, or make sure you clean everything after you finish eating. Like this, you can avoid procrastinating and can avoid ending up with a pile of dirty dishes, which you probably put off for days before you get yourself to clear that sink up.

If you are a woman with ADHD who shares a home with

a partner who likes to keep things organized, you might have ended up in a fight a couple of times because they misplaced your things in the name of tidying up. Then clearing your space does not necessarily mean they are helping you. You may struggle with finding things you put away, let alone when someone else does that for you. You have a lesser chance of findings things you are looking for when someone clears the space on your behalf. Try to always clear your things yourself, or if anyone else is helping you do that, make sure you agree on where things should go. You can encourage yourself to put things back by making things fancy and as attractive to get your attention as possible, but things will stay put only if they are practical to you. Make things easier to be put back and try to facilitate this process for yourself as much as possible.

Depending on how important that thing you just misplaced is, you are often going to feel anxious, stressed and annoyed when you lose it. Do your best to be organized; highlight, label, or decorate areas, so they get your attention and you can misplace things less often. If you often misplace small things like your wedding ring or watch, try keeping them in a bigger container like a bowl as soon as you walk in and out the door. Try to do one thing at a time because it has been established that people with ADHD struggle with multitasking, so this cannot help you find things when you lose them. If you need that set of keys because otherwise you cannot get out the door, try to ignore all other distractions, then focus only on finding the keys, try to recall where you placed them last and go look for them there. If you often misplace your stationery at work or home if you work remotely, try using a compact desk organizer so all your stationery items can stay collected in one place. Try making it a habit to clear your desk and place everything in your drawer before leaving at the end of the shift.

If you often misplace your phone, keys, watch and tablet, try introducing a docking station in your life. Leave it where you are most likely to leave the items that go on it. You can have all your valuables and electronics in one place and charged at one point. This way, you can lessen the times you walk out of the house with your phone uncharged. The chargers can all be at one place, and as soon as you walk in the house, you know where things have to go because you want them charged by the next morning too. You know where to look for things before walking out of the house as well. You can include compartments in the docking station to host things that do not necessarily need to be charged, like your house keys, your precious bullet journal and your glasses.

You may find it even harder to find things you do not use often. Say you have many small items you always use only for traveling, like your passport, your travel toothbrush, your luggage tag, or your padlocks. Try creating a space around the house that is dedicated to these items only. Keep everything in a visible container and label it or decorate it as you please.

If you wake up in the morning struggling to make a cup of coffee because everything is everywhere, try to create a designated area for coffee-making if this is something you often do and struggle with every day. There are plenty of fancy ideas online that will help you create a coffee station and make it a fun project. Try keeping your favorite mugs, a couple of spoons, coffee machine, tea, coffee and sugar in one place. The next time you need to make a coffee, it can be a breeze with this strategy.

If you have a project to deliver at work the next morning and need supplies to be taken to work, you can struggle to sleep at night knowing the things you must remember. Avoid the restless night and make a list. Gather all the things you know you will need and place them in your car, in your drive-in, or by the door. Collect everything you need to take with you, and if it helps, try making a list and leaving it where you can see it the next morning. This way, you can check off the things you need to take with you and avoid the anxiety or stress that comes with all of this. Although the last thing you feel like doing after a day at work or running errands is clearing the clutter or organizing your stuff, try making putting things back a habit and part of your routine. It can be difficult until you make this a habit.

Chapter 14: ADHD Woman and Pregnancy and Motherhood

Pregnant women who also have ADHD may report a drop in their ADHD symptoms. This is because estrogen levels spike during pregnancy. Estrogen targets the brain, helping with dopamine and other neurotransmitters. Keep in mind that ADHD is a spectrum and some symptoms may be more grievous in some individuals than others. Pregnancy and the estrogen fluctuations it brings with it might help lessen the ADHD symptoms, but that does not make it disappear completely or even cure it. Once pregnancy is over, estrogen levels will plummet again, causing ADHD symptoms to return, in some cases with more intensity—some report experiencing post-natal depression and anxiety. With becoming a parent, one must keep in mind this is a process and a life-changing event in itself, might we add. ADHD will impact you and your child whether you have it diagnosed or not.

Pregnancy and ADHD

Women may have a planned pregnancy, but some may get pregnant unexpectedly. Ideally, women with ADHD who also happen to be on medication for this condition would discuss and contemplate whether to stay on ADHD medication during pregnancy before getting pregnant. At this stage, women planning to get pregnant together with their physician and partner would weigh in the risks and benefits of getting pregnant and seizing ADHD medication versus continuing with treatment just the same. Women with ADHD who decide to alter or seize their ADHD medication may also need to continue doing so during breastfeeding. In most cases, this decision is taken after the woman learns she is pregnant, which would usually be four or more weeks into the pregnancy. At this stage, the fetus would have already been exposed to medication.

None of the treatments used in ADHD is proven to be safe in pregnant women, but there is no confirmation of them being unsafe either. There has never been an ethical way of conducting studies for the safety of such medication on pregnant women and the outcome on their babies to date. This leaves both physicians and expectant mothers at a crossroads. A physician would usually decide based on their knowledge, the documented outcomes of similar situations and their best judgment for their patient. They consider the woman with ADHD, the severity of her condition and other environmental variables. Seizing ADHD medication for a pregnant woman will affect her directly, her baby, her family and those around her. Because medication passes through the placenta and to the fetus, this will expose the baby to stimulant medication in the womb. Whether or not an expectant mother continues her ADHD treatment will be based heavily on her needs for the medication and her inclination to not expose her unborn baby to drugs that we know very little about when taken during pregnancy.

If an expectant mother with ADHD decides to stop her medication, those around her should be made aware. Symptoms of inattention, hyperactivity and impulsivity may return during pregnancy and when off medication. People at work, family members and friends may be taken off guard by this. They can also offer help and be your support system if you involve them in your decision. Decreasing your responsibilities during this time is beneficial. Women who take medication for their ADHD may find it difficult to transition to a period where they are off their medication and pregnant. Especially during maternity leave, expectant mothers tend to spend their last few days before giving birth at home. Staying at home a lot would not help, especially when you are off medication. Managing a business from home or doing simple house chores can also prove to be challenging without the help of your usual ADHD medication. ADHD treatment tends to build up in one's system, so once you stop the treatment, you would not experience symptoms straight away. This is subjective and depends on the dosage one would have been on before seizing treatment.

During the first months of pregnancy, a neurotypical woman would experience a stir of emotions caused by the pregnancy itself, so being a woman with ADHD who is also off her treatment may experience an even bigger emotional turmoil once the effects of the medication start to wear off. They may struggle with emotional overload and may also find it hard to control it. Pregnant women off treatment may feel tired, demotivated, experience suicidal thoughts and depression. When an ADHD brain has nothing to focus on or is not stimulated by anything, it may feel like shutting off, hence making the neurodiverse individual feel tired more often. Impulsivity may also be an issue for expectant mothers who stopped their ADHD treatment and so sticking to healthy eating practices and incorporating physical exercise may be slightly difficult to stick to.

If you are a woman with ADHD who just discovered that is pregnant and happen to be impulsive because of your ADHD, then it is best if you start adopting healthy eating habits to avoid impulse eating. This will help you avoid complications in pregnancy associated with your diet, like gestational diabetes. Setting time aside for food preparation can help with impulse eating as well. Make sure you make frequent grocery trips to ensure a good amount of healthy food is always available during your 9 months. Pre-natal vitamin intake is crucial during the first trimester and remembering to take your vitamins can be very challenging if you have ADHD. Try setting up alarms on your phone, have a stash of vitamins in areas you will remember to take them, like in your bag, at work and at home. Allow yourself to feel tired and permit yourself to rest because you are most definitely going to need it. Discuss budgeting ways with your partner, so you will not find yourself struggling to get the supplies you need at the very end of your pregnancy. If you are taking time off work and find yourself bored at home, try reading pregnancy books. With ADHD, it may be very easy to lose focus but reading about a stage you are going through at this very moment can help you keep your focus and teach you handy tips along the way. Socializing can also help you get the support you need from your family and friends whilst also enjoying some time out.

Motherhood and ADHD

Research and data on women with ADHD and breastfeeding on medication are lacking. ADHD treatment should only be taken if the potential benefit justifies the potential risk to the baby. Some physicians give a lot of importance to breastfeeding, which may vary from country to country as traditions tend to diversify. Doctors who emphasize breastfeeding and its benefits to the baby may encourage nursing mothers to discontinue any unnecessary medication as traces of these drugs may come up in the mother's milk. A physician may opt for short-acting medication for ADHD rather than a long-acting one. This will help the medication to peak quickly in the blood and last for a lesser amount of time. This can be achieved by switching from sustained-release medication to immediate-release medication. In these cases, the dosing schedule can be modified to fit the mother's and the baby's feeding and sleeping schedule. Immediate release medication can help reduce the exposure of treatment to the baby. With this treatment, drugs can peak for about two hours and will mean that during this time, the drug is highly present in the mother's blood and can be transferred easily to the baby during lactation. With sustained-release medication, the levels of medication in the blood rise at a slower pace and will remain available for longer, usually about 8 hours.

Choosing to lactate before taking the medication can work better with immediate-release medication but not sustained ones. Mothers may nurse their child before taking the dose, leaving a lessened possibility of passing the ADHD medication effects on the baby. This can become easier as the baby grows older as they tend to lactate less often, leaving the mother with a bigger window of availability for her to take her drugs. Because a baby's liver is less capable of breaking down medication, drugs secreted into the mother's breast milk can take longer to be cleared in a baby than in an adult. This makes the baby more susceptible to adverse drug effects. This will also depend on whether the baby is exclusively breastfeeding or also taking formula milk or solid foods. If this is the case, they would be taking less breastmilk and therefore are less exposed to traces of ADHD medication. If the mother opts to stay on ADHD medication while lactating, she may want to work closely with the pediatrician to monitor any reactions caused by the negative effects of her medication.

A parent may notice irritability, abnormal weight gain, agitation, changes in feeding habits and poor sleeping habits in their child. They must speak to their doctor and consider lowering the dose or stopping treatment altogether if this is the case. When a woman with ADHD decides to stop her treatment when she first becomes aware of her pregnancy, she might also be prepared to not take her medication at all, even after giving birth. Some physicians may ask expecting mothers to try getting off their medication whilst pregnant and allow them to start back on if they need to. If this is the case, then the mother may continue with ADHD medication throughout the pregnancy and follow through the nursing period as well. This will need to be discussed with your doctor to find the best possible solution for your condition and the baby.

Chapter 15: ADHD Woman and Postmenopausal

Menopause is a natural phase in a woman's life where her menstrual cycle eventually stops. Menopause can occur at different stages in a woman's life, and not everyone experiences it at the same age. A woman would go into menopause primarily because her ovaries have stopped producing hormones, mainly estrogen and progesterone. Testosterone levels, the follicle-stimulating hormone, also known as FSH and luteinizing hormone, also known as LH, also fluctuate during menopause. A woman is thought to reach menopause when she fails to have a menstrual cycle for one year. Estrogen levels are said to drop drastically during this period, and those going through this phase may experience irregular menstrual cycles, hot flushes, vaginal dryness, mood swings and trouble sleeping. These symptoms are experienced by most women regardless of whether they suffer from ADHD or not. But having ADHD surely does not help to get through this natural event. Menopause may at times be induced in cases of surgical removal of the ovaries, pelvic radiation, or hormone therapy. Blood tests can be a way of knowing whether you have entered the perimenopausal stages, whereby you would experience lighter symptoms of menopause. Menopause is also associated with osteoporosis, fractures, changes in cognitive behavior, mood changes and loss of libido. Measuring levels of hormones in the blood can help determine whether you are currently going through menopause.

Women who have ADHD and start getting into menopause confess experiencing confusion, difficulty multitasking, memory struggles and general cognitive difficulties. Some might suspect developing Alzheimer's or dementia. Someone who is already on ADHD medication and was controlling their condition may find that whatever used to work just fine for their ADHD may not be sufficient when menopause hits. This is because ADHD combined with lower levels of estrogen can cause an overwhelming feeling. Women who get diagnosed with ADHD at a later stage might experience regret and remorse when looking back at the things they could have achieved if they got the help and treatment they deserved. They would have suffered fewer years of self-abuse and treating themselves as if they were complete failures, lazy and stupid.

Estrogen affects the release of serotonin. This is the key hormone that stabilizes your mood and helps your brain cells to communicate. This will affect digestion, sleeping and eating habits. You can help increase levels of serotonin in the brain naturally; by exposing yourself a little more often to bright light, exercise, meditation, getting massages and consuming certain foods. Serotonin is not readily available in food sources but is found in its amino acid form, tryptophan which is converted into serotonin in the brain. Consuming nuts, seeds, spinach, salmon and eggs can help increase tryptophan levels naturally. Low levels of estrogen during menopause causes even lower levels of dopamine in the brain, exacerbating the symptoms of ADHD. Certain treatments that would usually or mostly work for college students with ADHD may no longer be as effective for menopausal women with ADHD. This is because the decrease in dopamine stems from hormones and not from ADHD. Controlling your ADHD can be crucial in women with perimenopausal symptoms. If your ADHD is not controlled, it will be very difficult to identify the issue and why you are experiencing such symptoms. If your ADHD is controlled, then one can easily rule it out as the root cause of your current symptoms. Increasing ADHD medication will not help in these cases because nothing is being done for low estrogen levels.

One would hope that by the time you reach menopause, you would have also received adequate treatment for your ADHD. At this point, your ADHD is controlled, but minimizing the symptoms of menopause can help control your ADHD as well. It is suggested that loose, layered and light clothing is worn to help manage hot flushes. Avoiding heavy blankets and keeping the bedroom cool can also help with this. If you experience hot flushes even during the day, try carrying a small portable fan to help with this. Regular exercise can help with increasing energy, promote better sleep and improve your mood. Physical activity, even for 30 minutes daily, can help promote general well-being and help control your weight. If you are experiencing massive mood changes and going through periodic episodes of depression or anxiety, speak to a therapist and make sure your family members or loved ones are aware of what you are going through. Vitamins can help to supplement your diet during menopause. Calcium, Magnesium and vitamin D supplements can help reduce the occurrence of osteoporosis or slow its progression. This will also improve sleep and energy levels. If you are experiencing sleep issues, try consulting a professional to help control your sleeping patterns. Irregularities in melatonin production can cause depression, but in the right amounts, it can help create a healthy sleeping pattern. Yoga and meditation can also help ease stress. Because during menopause, women tend to experience skin dryness, it is suggested that moisturizers are used daily. Avoiding excessive bathing or swimming can help lessen skin dryness and irritation.

If you feel like completing certain tasks at work has become a challenge, try bartering them with someone else at the office. If you forget to make phone calls daily, try asking a colleague if she can complete them for you, and in exchange, you can do some of her tasks. Try finding the root cause for what is making you forget or avoid making phone calls. You may want to keep a clean working area to avoid clutter and confusion. Prepare for phone calls before making them, so you avoid forgetting what you need to say. If emails work better for you, try encouraging your clients to contact you via email. If you can delegate more work to ease the workload, go ahead and do it. Do not feel like a failure because you are not doing everything on your own; you should not. You need to understand that those around you are part of your support system and are there to share your burden. If what you need to work better is a strategy, use the help of those around you to set one up. If you feel like you already have too much work, learn to say no to new responsibilities or negotiate a better deadline. Writing to-do lists will help you get into the right mind frame for the day. If your day is over and you know you have left so many unfinished tasks, try jotting them down one by one in order of importance and priority. Once you have that done, clear the clutter to start afresh the next day.

With a to-do list set, your day is already planned and will help you stay focused longer. Strike things off the list when you are done, and keep with this habit if it works for you. If one task is complicated or you are sure you will not complete it the next day, divide it into smaller tasks and try completing those mini-tasks to keep up with goals and deadlines. If you work in a dynamic office environment where your superiors fire duties and tasks to you as they make their morning coffee in the staff canteen. You will be able to write down tasks, instructions and deadlines when this happens. If you feel unsure about the goal objectives, try asking your boss to email you the assignment in detail later so you can have something to look back to while completing the assignment and be sure you do not miss any important details.

Although this tip may not work for everyone, it can help to take it under consideration. You may want to hire a professional organizer who will help you declutter your space and keep you accountable. Cognitive behavior therapy can also help in increasing self-control and self-esteem, two factors negatively impacted during menopause.

Menopause cannot be avoided, but by keeping track of any menstrual changes, mood changes and sleep disturbances, you will soon start to notice these changes and have a record of them. This will give you an indication of where you stand, and with that information at hand, you can discuss your ADHD symptoms and menopausal ones with your psychiatrist, therapist, gynecologist, or physician. ADHD will not disappear with time but knowing how to manage it based on the different stages of life is key to keep it under control.